D0807769

097013

Teach Yourself®

Get Started in Windows 7

Mac Bride

For UK order enquiries: please contact Bookpoint Ltd,
130 Milton Park, Abingdon, Oxon OX14 4SB.
Telephone: +44 (0) 1235 827720. Fax: +44 (0) 1235 400454.
Lines are open 09.00–17.00, Monday to Saturday, with a 24-hour
message answering service. Details about our titles and how to
order are available at www.teachyourself.com

For USA order enquiries: please contact McGraw-Hill Customer
Services, PO Box 545, Blacklick, OH 43004-0545, USA.
Telephone: 1-800-722-4726. Fax: 1-614-755-5645.

For Canada order enquiries: please contact McGraw-Hill Ryerson
Ltd, 300 Water St, Whitby, Ontario L1N 9B6, Canada.
Telephone: 905 430 5000. Fax: 905 430 5020.

Long renowned as the authoritative source for self-guided learning –
with more than 50 million copies sold worldwide – the **Teach Yourself**
series includes over 500 titles in the fields of languages, crafts, hobbies,
business, computing and education.

British Library Cataloguing in Publication Data: a catalogue record
for this title is available from the British Library.

Library of Congress Catalog Card Number: on file.

First published in UK 2010 by Hodder Education, part of Hachette
UK, 338 Euston Road, London NW1 3BH.

First published in US 2010 by The McGraw-Hill Companies, Inc.

The **Teach Yourself** name is a registered trade mark of
Hodder Headline.

Typeset by MPS Limited, A Macmillan Company.

Printed in Great Britain for Hodder Education, an Hachette UK
Company, 338 Euston Road, London NW1 3BH, by CPI Cox &
Wyman, Reading, Berkshire RG1 8EX.

The publisher has used its best endeavours to ensure that the URLs
for external websites referred to in this book are correct and active
at the time of going to press. However, the publisher and the
author have no responsibility for the websites and can make no
guarantee that a site will remain live or that the content will remain
relevant, decent or appropriate.

Hachette UK's policy is to use papers that are natural, renewable
and recyclable products and made from wood grown in sustainable
forests. The logging and manufacturing processes are expected to
conform to the environmental regulations of the country of origin.

Impression number   10 9 8 7 6 5 4 3 2 1
Year   2014 2013 2012 2011 2010

Contents

Welcome to *Teach Yourself Windows 7*!

Windows 7 is the latest version of Microsoft's world beating operating system, and one that takes another step further along the path of making computers easier to use. It is highly graphic, so that you can see what you are doing. It offers very efficient and effective ways of storing files – it's great for managing your digital photos and music. It's designed for online life and for linking to others through the Internet and/or through a network in the office or at home. I've been working with Windows since the first working (well, almost working) version, and this is the best yet.

Working with Windows is intuitive – once you know how to 'intuit'! When you have mastered the basics and become familiar with some applications, you should be able to apply your understanding of the 'Windows way' to any other Windows applications that interest you.

Happy Windowing.

Mac Bride

Southampton, 2009

Only got one minute?

This book introduces the basic concepts of working with Windows (the system) and windows (the framed parts of the screen in which programs run). It will show you how to set up your computer to suit the way you like to work – you can control more or less everything from the screen display down to the speed of the mouse's response! You will find out how to manage your files efficiently, organizing your storage so that you can find things quickly and removing unwanted clutter, and how to care for your disks so they continue to perform well for a long time.

The Windows package includes many accessories and applications, both large and small. We will be looking briefly at some of these, and more closely at Internet Explorer and Live Mail. With these two tools you can browse and download files from the Internet, and handle e-mail. Windows 7 has been designed for easy Internet access, in fact, integration with the Internet is central to its design. If you choose, and if you have the hardware and the connections to support it, you can almost treat the Internet as an extension of your Desktop.

This book does not aim to cover every single aspect of Windows 7, for two very good reasons. First, there is far too much to fit into 320 pages, and second, few people will ever use all its features. *Get Started in Windows 7* concentrates on the needs of the new user at home and in the office. It aims to cover the things that you need to know to be able to use your computer efficiently, and things that you might like to know because they can make using your computer more enjoyable. If you later want to learn how to get more out of your PC and/or set up a network for the PCs in your home or business, have a look at *Teach Yourself Get to Grips with PC Networking*.

5 Only got five minutes?

Computers don't bite, or kick or scream. The worst they can do is beep at you, or stop working while you are in the middle of doing something. (That doesn't happen very often with Windows 7, and if it does you can normally get back to where you were in a few minutes.) What this means is that you can feel free to try things out. When you meet something new – an application that you are using for the first time, or a feature that you haven't used before – play with it. For example, if you want to edit a digital photo to improve the colour or create a special effect, experiment with the sample pictures or your own 'woops-what-happened-there' snaps (and we all have lots of those) before you try it on your only photo of Great Aunt Edna.

Windows 7 is basically a point-and-click system. To start a program or activity, to set an option or to select an object, you normally point at and click on the appropriate icon (little graphic) on the screen – either using the mouse, or the touchpad on a laptop, or the screen itself if it is touch-sensitive. (You can use the keyboard to do these things, but it's not ideal.) It's often obvious what an icon does, either from the picture itself or a label beside it. With some others, if you wait a moment a box will pop up and tell you what the icon is for. Overall, it's generally fairly obvious what you can do at any point, and you can do it – whatever it is – by clicking. You will normally click using the left button, and just give a single click on it. Sometimes you double-click and sometimes you click the right button, and you'll see when and where later.

Try it. If you machine isn't turned on now, turn it on. There will be some icons on the screen. Click on one and see what happens. Look at the bottom left corner of the screen. That round icon with the Windows logo is the Start button. Click on that and you can get to any program or document anywhere on the PC. Try clicking on names and icons there and see what happens.

WordPad ▸	Mac
Skype	Documents
Paint ▸	Pictures
Windows Live Mail	Music
Microsoft Office Word 2007 ▸	Games ▸
RealPlayer	Computer
Notepad ▸	Control Panel
Windows Live Photo Gallery ▸	Devices and Printers
Windows Media Center	Default Programs
Desktop Gadget Gallery	Help and Support
Sticky Notes ▸	
Calculator	
▸ All Programs	
Search programs and files 🔍	Sleep ▸

All this clicking is probably cluttering up your screen with stuff that you don't really want. No problem. Look at the top right corner of any window (the part of the screen that a program is running in) and you will see a button labelled X. Point to it and the button will turn red. Click on it and the window will close.

Try it! Click on icons. Run some programs, get some windows open. Then close them again. If you can start and stop things, you are in control. Start to take control of your PC now.

When you've had enough – or if you think that things are getting out of control – then click the Start button again, point to the arrow on the button at the bottom right, and click on Shut down.

If for any reason that doesn't do the job – sometimes computers can get confused too – then turn it off at its switch.

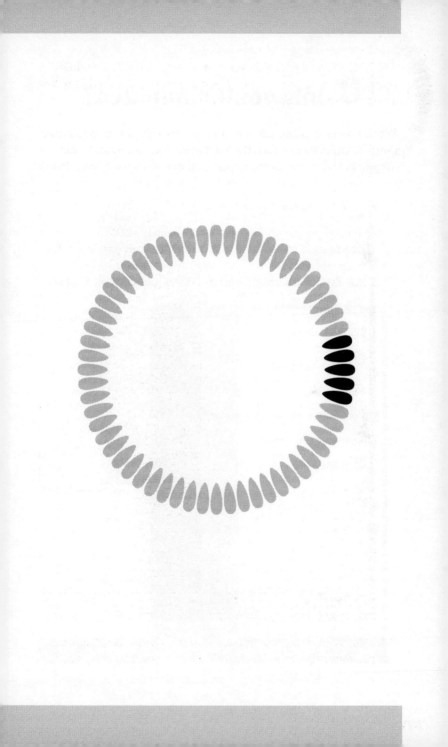

10 Only got ten minutes?

10 minutes isn't really long enough to cover all you need to know about Windows 7 – even in a very potted form – but it is long enough to show you just how easy a Windows 7 computer is to use, so that's what I'm going to do. Follow the steps.

1 Turn the PC (or laptop) on.
2 If several people use the machine, you may need to log on – click the icon with your name, and enter your password if you are asked for it.
3 Click the Start button. Point to Games and click on Solitaire.

4 This is a standard patience game. The normal rules apply. Click on the pack to turn over cards. Build red-black-red down on the seven exposed cards. When you find aces, move them to the top area, then build their suits up on them. To move a card, click on it, hold down the left mouse button, and drag it to where you want it to go, then release the button.

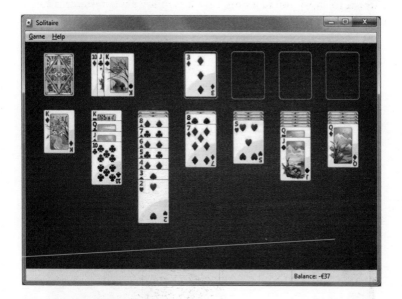

5 Play until you've got the hang of it, and then go on to the next step – we've only got 10 minutes here, you know!

6 Leave the Solitaire game running, so that you can come back to it when you have finished here. It's time to do some word processing!

WordPad is the word processor that is supplied with Windows 7. It's a simple one – by today's standards – but has all that you need for writing and formatting letters, essays, reports, or even a best-selling novel (though you have to provide the story and characters yourself!). WordPad is one of a number of accessories – applications included in the Windows package. You can run it from the Start menu.

1 Click the Start button, then click All Programs, down at the bottom on the left.

A≣ WordPad ▸		
S Skype	Mac	
🎨 Paint ▸	Documents	
Windows Live Mail	Pictures	
W≣ Microsoft Office Word 2007 ▸	Music	
Windows Live Photo Gallery ▸	Games ▸	
℗ RealPlayer	Computer	
Notepad ▸	Control Panel	
Windows Media Center	Devices and Printers	
Desktop Gadget Gallery	Default Programs	
Sticky Notes ▸	Help and Support	
Calculator		
▸ All Programs		
Search programs and files 🔎	Sleep ▸	

2 Click Accessories – this is a folder that contains links to several programs, and we need to open it.

Adobe Reader 9	
Default Programs	Mac
Desktop Gadget Gallery	
Internet Explorer	Documents
Windows DVD Maker	
Windows Fax and Scan	Pictures
Windows Media Center	
Windows Media Player	Music
Windows Update	
XPS Viewer	Games ▸
Accessories	
Games	Computer
Maintenance	
Microsoft Office	Control Panel
QuickTime	
Real	Devices and Printers
Skype	
Startup	Default Programs
Windows Live	
	Help and Support

◀ Back

Search programs and files 🔎   Sleep ▸

3 Click WordPad at the bottom of the list of programs in the Accessories set.

Windows Update
XPS Viewer
Accessories
   Calculator
   Command Prompt
   Connect to a Network Projector
   Connect to a Projector
   Getting Started
   Math Input Panel
   Notepad
   Paint
   Remote Desktop Connection
   Run
   Snipping Tool
   Sound Recorder
   Sticky Notes
   Sync Center
   Windows Explorer
   Windows Mobility Center
   WordPad
   Ease of Access
   System Tools
   Tablet PC
   Windows PowerShell

Back

Search programs and files

Mac

Documents

Pictures

Music

Games

Computer

Control Panel

Devices and Printers

Default Programs

Help and Support

Sleep

4 The WordPad window will open, and give you a blank sheet to start typing on. Here is all you need to know to type and enter text in WordPad.

Instant WordPad

The flashing line mark into the new place with the insertion point – where text will go if you start typing. It travels ahead of you as you type.

You may need to move it to correct mistakes or add more text further back. To move it either click where you want it to go, or use the arrow keys.

To remove mistakes, either:

press the **Backspace** key to delete to the left of the insertion point (i.e. the characters you have just typed)
or
press the **Delete** key to delete characters to the right of the insertion point.

You can use either key to delete selected text, as you will see in Chapter 4.

You can change the size, font, colour, alignment and other aspects of text – but that will take more than 10 minutes to explain!

1 Start to type something – anything! It could be the first page of your next novel, or a letter to Uncle Louis, or some notes on how to use WordPad, or a shopping list.

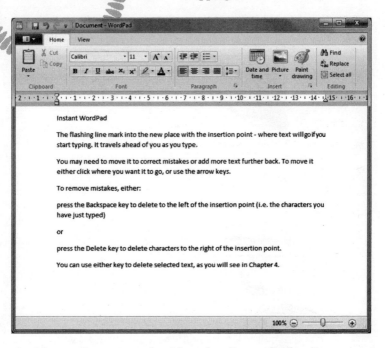

2 After you've written the title or heading and a few lines, save your work as a file. You can then come back and add more to it later, when you have time.

3 Click the WordPad button – up at the top left, beneath the thick top frame. A menu will drop down from it. Click on Save As.

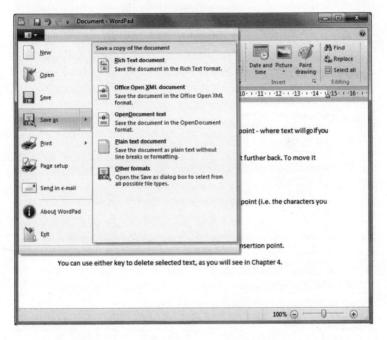

4 In the File Name slot type a name that will identify the file. Don't worry about anything else here – it will be saved in your documents area, where you will be able to find it later.

5 Click the button labelled Save.

6 Click the X button in the top right of the window to close WordPad – in Chapter 4 I'll show you how to reopen that file so that you can get back to work on it.

That's it. Your 10 minutes is up. Think of what you have achieved in that short time. You have set two programs running, learned to drag and drop with the mouse, to type and edit text, to save a file and to close down a program.

Now, if you followed the steps exactly, you should still have Solitaire running, so if you've got time to spare, why not finish the game. It's good mouse practice.

1

Introducing Windows 7

Experienced user?

If you have previously used any similar computer system –
such as an earlier version of Windows or Apple Macintosh –
skim through the next few pages, or skip them altogether,
and go straight to Chapter 2.

1.1 What is Windows 7?

Windows 7 is an *operating system* – and more. An operating
system handles the low-level interaction between the processor
and the screen, memory, mouse, disk drives, printer and other
peripherals. Windows 7 has *drivers* (control programs) for all
PC-compatible processors and for most of the PC peripherals on
the market – though in the first year or so after launch there will
be some older peripherals that may not work with Windows 7 as
their drivers are still being developed.

An operating system is a bridge between the hardware of the
computer and its *applications* – such as word processors and
spreadsheets. As a result, whatever PC you have and whoever
made it, as long as it can run the Windows 7 operating system,
it can run any Windows 7 application. (It will also be able to run
applications written for earlier versions of Windows.)

Although the operating system is the most important part of
Windows, most of it is invisible to you. You don't even need to

think about how it works or what it does as Windows 7 has its own routines for checking and maintaining the operating system.

THE DESKTOP

The most visible part of Windows is, of course, the screen or *Desktop*. Windows uses *icons* (small images) to represent programs and files, and visual displays to show what is happening inside your PC. Many of the routine jobs are done by clicking on, dragging or otherwise manipulating these images, using the mouse or keyboard.

Windows is *multi-tasking* – it can run any number of programs at once. In practice, only a few will normally be active at the same time but that is more a reflection of the human inability to do several jobs simultaneously! A typical example of multi-tasking would be one program downloading material from the Internet, another playing a CD, a third printing a long report, while you wrote a letter in a fourth.

Each program runs in a separate area of the screen – a window – and these can be resized, moved, minimized or overlapped however you like. Managing windows is covered in Chapter 3.

UTILITIES AND ACCESSORIES

Apart from the operating system, Windows 7 contains a number of programs. Some of these are utilities for managing the system – organizing file storage on the disk, adding new peripherals or fine-tuning the way that they work. Others are applications for your use and amusement. You've got WordPad, a good word processor, Media Player for playing downloaded music files, CDs and DVDs, a calculator, some games, a set of multimedia tools and applications for the Internet, including Internet Explorer, and a bunch of gadgets for livening up your Desktop.

There is a second set of applications, called Live Essentials, which are intended for use with Windows 7 but have not been packaged with it – you need to download them from the Internet. These include Live Messenger, an instant messaging service that runs across the Internet, Live Mail, for sending and receiving messages by e-mail, Photo Gallery, for displaying images from your digital camera, and Movie Maker, for editing home videos. You will find out how to download and install them in Chapter 8 – it's free, simple and takes only a few moments.

All of the essential utilities and the more useful applications are covered in this book.

INTEGRATION WITH THE INTERNET

Windows 7 offers a high level of integration with the Internet – it can become almost an extension of your Desktop. Integration works best if your PC is connected to the Internet through a broadband line, giving fast, easy access. A dial-up connection is OK if all you want to do is e-mail and a little Web browsing from time to time but for anything else it is far too slow.

Author's tip!
At the time of writing, 90% of the UK population has access to a broadband connection, and full coverage should be reached by 2012. If you are still using a dial-up line, upgrade to broadband as soon as you can.

MULTIPLE USERS

Under Windows, a PC can be set up for multiple users. Each user will have their own space on the hard disk for storing files and can customize the look and feel of the PC to suit themselves.

Plug and Play
These built-in control routines come into play when you add new hardware, such as a joystick, printer or extra hard drive, to your PC. Windows 7 will normally recognize their presence automatically, and install the software needed to control them. The 'plug and play' approach makes it easy to add peripherals to your system.

1.2 The Desktop

The screen should be treated as if it really were a desktop. This is where you keep your tools – utilities and applications – and you can arrange things so that those tools you use most often are close at hand. This is where you create your documents – and you may have several under way at the same time, in the same or in separate applications. You can arrange these so that you can read two or more at once if you want to compare them or to copy material from one to another. If you have finished with an application for the time being, you can tuck it out of the way – but it is still ready to be restarted with a click of the mouse.

WHAT'S ON THE DESKTOP?

What do you see when you look at the screen? The answer will vary, of course, depending upon what you are doing and how you have set up the system, but some or all of these items should be visible.

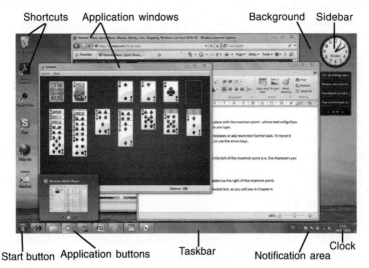

Figure 1.1 The Desktop showing some of the main features.

Background

This may be a flat colour, a pattern, or one or more pictures or photographs – you can have a set of images that change constantly,

4

so that every time you see the background, there's something different to look at. The background display can be changed at any time without affecting anything else.

Shortcuts

These are icons with links to programs, documents, *folders* (for storing files on the hard disk) or places on the Internet. Clicking on the icon will run the program, open the document in the appropriate program, open the folder or take you off into the Internet. There are some shortcuts there already, more are available (see page 93) and you can add your own (see page 123).

Taskbar

This is normally present as a strip along the bottom of the screen, but can be moved elsewhere (Chapter 11). It is the control centre for the Desktop, carrying the tools and buttons to start and to switch between applications.

Programs that you use regularly can be pinned to the Taskbar so that they are always at hand.

Start button

Clicking on the **Start** button opens the Start menu.
Any application on your system can be run from here. You can also use it to open any documents or files that you have been working on recently, and to access the Help and Support centre and other utilities.

NOTIFICATION AREA

This holds icons for a variety of mainly system programs. The volume control is also here.

Clock

This is optional, but useful. The clock keeps excellent time – it even adjusts itself at the start and end of Daylight Saving Time!

Show Desktop

If you point to the little blank rectangle at the extreme right of the Taskbar, the application windows will become transparent so that you can see the Desktop underneath – and you can also see from the outlines how many windows you have open.

If you click on the Show Desktop button, it shrinks all open applications out of the way so that you have a clear view of the Desktop.

Show desktop

Figure 1.2 Pointing to show Desktop lets you see through the windows!

Application windows

When you run an application, such as Windows Explorer (Chapter 8), WordPad, or Paint (both in Chapter 12), it opens in a window. This can be set to fill the screen or to take up a smaller area so that part of the Desktop is visible beneath (see Chapter 3 for more on windows).

Application buttons

When you run an application, a button is added to the Taskbar. If you point to this button, you will see a thumbnail image of the application's window. Clicking it will bring the application to the front of the Desktop.

GADGETS AND THE SIDEBAR

On the right of the Desktop is the Sidebar where you can display your 'gadgets'. There are about a dozen of these supplied in the Windows package, and more are available online. They include a clock (and you can have any number of these, each set to a different time zone), a calendar, your contacts lists and utilities that will pull headlines, share prices or weather information off the Internet. We'll look at gadgets in Chapter 6.

Customizing the Desktop

The appearance of the Desktop and the way that you interact with it can be changed to suit yourself (see Chapter 6).

1.3 The mouse

The mouse is almost essential for work with Windows – you can manage without it, but not as easily. It is used for selecting and manipulating objects, highlighting text, making choices, and clicking icons and buttons – as well as for drawing in graphics applications. There are five key 'moves'.

Point
The easy one! Move the mouse so that the tip of the arrow cursor (or the finger of the hand cursor) is over the object you want to point to. If you point to an icon, and hold the cursor there for a moment, a label will appear, telling you what the icon stands for. If you reach the edge of the mouse mat before the pointer has reached its target, pick the mouse up and put it down again in the middle of the mat.

Click
A single click of the left button will select an object or position the cursor in a block of text.

Right-click
A single click of the right button will open a shortcut menu.

Double-click
Two clicks, in quick succession, of the left button will start a program or open a document. You can adjust the double-click speed (see page 212).

Drag
Point to an object or place on the Desktop, hold down the left mouse button and draw the cursor across the screen.

1.4 The keyboard

The keyboard is mainly for entering and editing text, but can also be used for controlling the system. Note these keys:

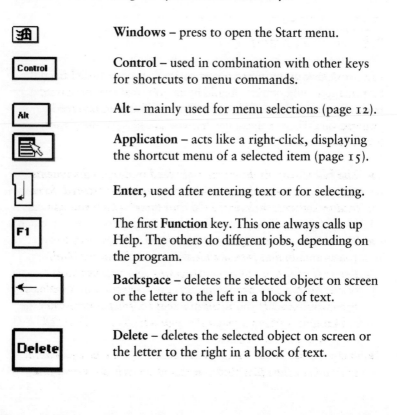

Windows – press to open the Start menu.

Control – used in combination with other keys for shortcuts to menu commands.

Alt – mainly used for menu selections (page 12).

Application – acts like a right-click, displaying the shortcut menu of a selected item (page 15).

Enter, used after entering text or for selecting.

The first **Function** key. This one always calls up Help. The others do different jobs, depending on the program.

Backspace – deletes the selected object on screen or the letter to the left in a block of text.

Delete – deletes the selected object on screen or the letter to the right in a block of text.

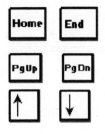

Jump to the start/end of a line, or the top/bottom of a block of text or a window display.

Scroll up/down one window length.

Move through text, menus and folder displays. Can often be combined with `Control` for faster movement.

Easier access

If you find either the mouse or keyboard difficult to use, the options in the Ease of Access Center may be able to help. See page 217.

1.5 The Start menu

Any work that you want to do on your PC can be started from the Start menu (see Figure 1.3) – and many jobs can also be started from elsewhere, as you will see. The menu has been designed to give you quick access to things that you are likely to need most. It has three areas:

▶ *The black buttons down the right lead mainly to documents, or rather to the folders in which documents are stored. Some lead to utilities, such as the Control Panel which you can use to configure Windows.*

▶ *The entries on the right are to programs. At the very top you normally find Internet Explorer and Windows Mail. Below them are listed those programs that you use most often. (At the very beginning, there is a selection of Windows programs here.) If you want one that isn't listed here, clicking* All Programs *opens a menu through which every installed application can be reached.*

▶ *If a program name has an arrow on its right, when you point to it, a list of the files that you recently worked on with that program will appear. Click on the filename to open it and run the program.*

▶ *In the strip across the bottom are the shut-down options and a special search facility.*

We'll come back to the use of the Start menu in Chapter 2, and in Chapter 11 look at ways of customizing it.

Figure 1.3 The Start menu as it first appears – you will probably have a different selection of application links on the left.

The smart Start menu

The Start menu learns as you work. It displays the programs that you use most often, and will change this if you start to use other programs more, and it constantly updates the lists of recently-used files for each program.

1.6 Menus in applications

In many current and in most older Windows applications, the commands and options are usually grouped on a set of pull-down menus. They follow simple rules:

▶ *If an item has an* ▶ *on the right, a submenu will open when you point to the item.*

▶ *If an item has ... after the name, a dialog box (page 16) will open when you point to the item, to collect information.*

▶ *If an item has* ⚫ *to its left, it is the selected option from a set.*

▶ *If an item has* ✓ *to its left, it is an option and is turned on – click to turn it off or on again.*

▶ *If a name is in grey ('greyed out'), the command is not available at that time – you probably have to first select something that it can be applied to.*

Conversation		
Send	▶	
Extras	▶	
Profile	▶	⚫ Small
Remove from Contacts		Large
Add People...		Hide
Rename...		
Leave Conversation		
Block...		
Notification Settings...		
Find...	Ctrl+F	
View Old Messages		
Mark as Unread		
Remove from Conversations List		
Recently Closed Conversations	▶	

Figure 1.4 A typical application menu – this is in Skype.

MENUS AND THE MOUSE

▶ *To open a menu, click on its name in the Menu bar.*
▶ *To run a command or set an option, click on it with the mouse.*
▶ *To leave the menu system without selecting a command, click anywhere else on the screen.*

MENU SELECTION USING THE KEYBOARD

When the work that you are doing is mainly typing, you may find it more convenient to make your menu selections via the keyboard. Here's how:

1 *Hold down* [**Alt**] *and press the underlined letter in the name on the Menu bar.*
2 *Press the underlined letter of the name to run the command, set the on/off option or open the submenu.*

Or

3 *Move through the menus with the arrow keys – up/down the menu and right to open submenus – then press* [**Enter**].
▶ *The left/right arrows will move you from one menu to another.*
▶ *Press* [**Escape**] *to close the menu without selecting a command.*

KEYBOARD SHORTCUTS

Many applications allow you to run some of the most commonly-used commands directly from the keyboard, without touching the menu system. For example, in many applications, [**Control**] + [S] (i.e. hold down the [**Control**] key and press [S]) will call up the Save command; [**Control**] + [O] has the same effect as selecting **Open** from the **File** menu.

The shortcuts vary, and some applications will offer far more than others, but some are common to all – or most – applications. If a command has a keyboard shortcut, it will be shown on the menu, to the right of the name.

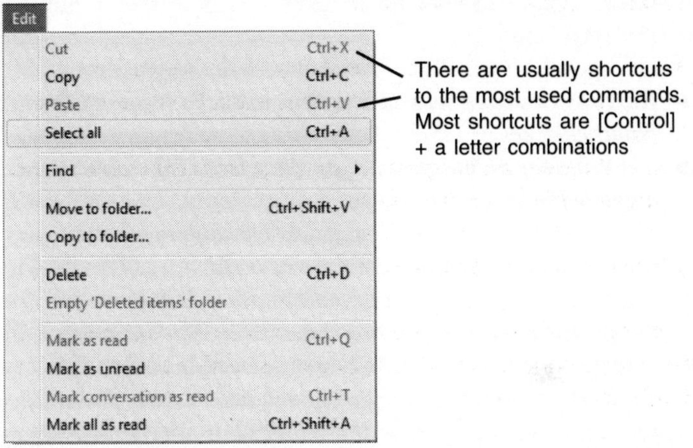

Edit	
Cut	Ctrl+X
Copy	Ctrl+C
Paste	Ctrl+V
Select all	Ctrl+A
Find	▶
Move to folder...	Ctrl+Shift+V
Copy to folder...	
Delete	Ctrl+D
Empty 'Deleted items' folder	
Mark as read	Ctrl+Q
Mark as unread	
Mark conversation as read	Ctrl+T
Mark all as read	Ctrl+Shift+A

There are usually shortcuts to the most used commands. Most shortcuts are [Control] + a letter combinations

Figure 1.5 A menu showing keyboard shortcuts.

Learn some shortcuts

It's worth learning the keyboard shortcuts for the commands that you use most often. When you are typing, it's much quicker to use the keyboard than the mouse.

1.7 Ribbons and the main menu

Microsoft introduced a new way of selecting commands in Office 2007, and has used this in some of the applications in the Windows 7 package. Instead of a menu bar (which gives access to all the commands in the application) and a toolbar (which has shortcuts to the ones people use most), they put the commands onto a Ribbon, and a single main menu. The Ribbon holds those that are used for working on the document – or picture, or whatever, e.g. to set the size of text or to change a colour. The main menu holds those that affect the document as a whole, e.g. opening, closing and saving files.

We will be looking at Ribbons in several programs later, but these points always apply:

- ▶ *Ribbons can have several layers or tabs. To bring a tab to the front, click on its label.*
- ▶ *The commands and options are all accessed through tools, arranged in groups.*
- ▶ *If a tool has no options, e.g. it sets left alignment, or turns bold on or off, then just click on it.*
- ▶ *If a tool has options or alternatives, there will be an arrow beside or below it. Click the arrow to see the options.*
- ▶ *If there are commands which are too complicated to be handled by tools, then the group will have a dialog box. Click the dialog box launcher in the group's bottom right corner to open this.*

In Ribbon systems, the menu is opened from a button up at the top left.

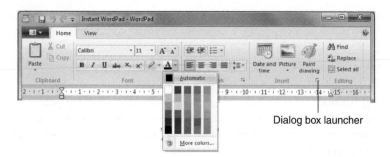

Dialog box launcher

Figure 1.6 The Ribbon in WordPad.

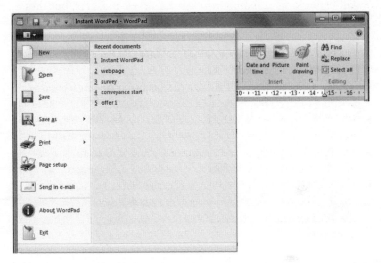

Figure 1.7 The menu in WordPad. Recently used files are listed on the right – if you point to a command with options, they are displayed in this area.

1.8 Shortcut menus

If you right-click on more or less anything on the screen – a file icon, a piece of text, a picture, the Desktop – or press the **Application** key when an object is selected, a menu will appear beside or on the object. This is its *shortcut* or *context menu* – it will contain a set of commands and options that are relevant to the object in that context.

Right-click on a shortcut to a folder, on a shortcut to an application, on the Taskbar or on the background and see what comes up. Don't worry at this stage about what the commands and options do, just notice how they vary – and that some are present on many menus.

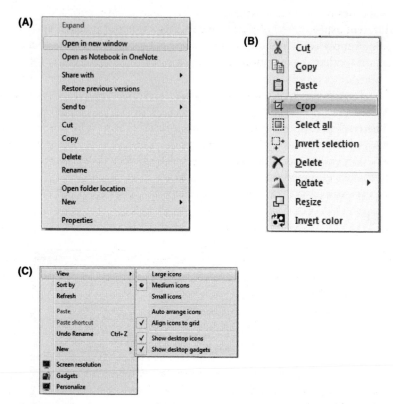

Figure 1.8 Three examples of shortcut menus, from (A) a folder in Windows Explorer, (B) a selected area in Paint and (C) the Desktop.

1.9 Properties, dialog boxes and options

Almost every object in the Windows system has *Properties*, which define what it looks like and how it works. These can be seen, and often changed, through the Properties panel. This is normally reached through the context menu – you will see that menu A in Figure 1.8 has **Properties** as the last item (and **Personalize** in menu C also leads to several Properties panels).

Properties panels often have several *tabs*, each dealing with a different aspect of the object. The contents vary enormously. Some simply contain information – such as the size, date and other details – others have options that you can set in different ways.

▶ To *switch between tabs, click on the name at the top.*

When a Windows program wants to get information from you, it will do it through a *panel* or *dialog box*. These vary in size and style, depending upon the information to be collected. Windows uses a range of methods for setting options and collecting information in its Properties panels and dialog boxes.

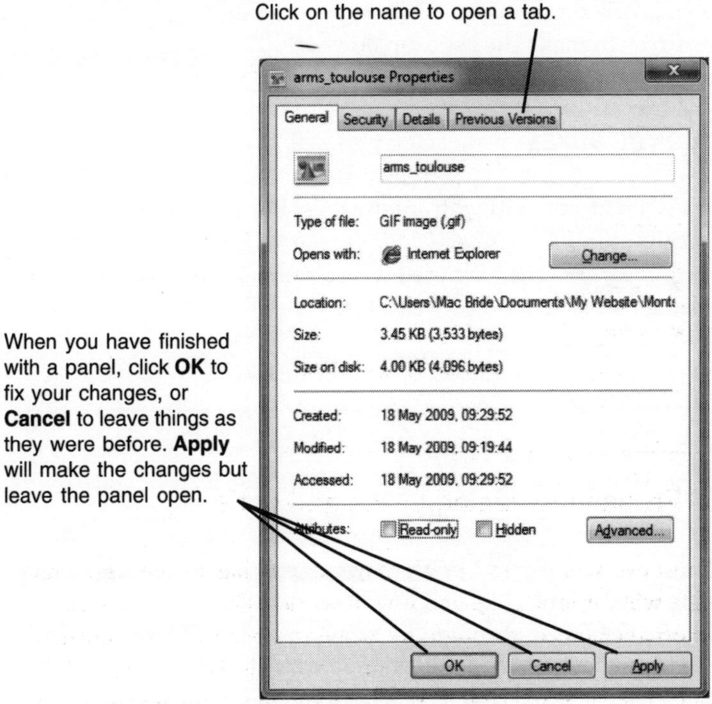

Click on the name to open a tab.

When you have finished with a panel, click **OK** to fix your changes, or **Cancel** to leave things as they were before. **Apply** will make the changes but leave the panel open.

arms_toulouse Properties

General | Security | Details | Previous Versions

arms_toulouse

Type of file: GIF image (.gif)

Opens with: Internet Explorer   Change...

Location: C:\Users\Mac Bride\Documents\My Website\Monts

Size: 3.45 KB (3,533 bytes)

Size on disk: 4.00 KB (4,096 bytes)

Created: 18 May 2009, 09:29:52

Modified: 18 May 2009, 09:19:44

Accessed: 18 May 2009, 09:29:52

Attributes: ☐ Read-only   ☐ Hidden   Advanced...

OK   Cancel   Apply

Figure 1.9 The Properties panel for an image file. Some data can be changed on the Properties panel; other things can only be set by the system.

TEXT BOXES

Typically used for collecting filenames or personal details. Sometimes a value will be suggested by the system. Edit it, or retype it if necessary.

DROP-DOWN LISTS

In Windows utilities and applications, drop-down lists look like buttons; in older software they are more like text boxes. They can be recognized by a down arrow on the right. Click on the arrow to make the list drop down, then select a value.

COMBO BOXES

This is a text box with a drop-down list built in, and the list typically stores names, web addresses or other data that you typed in earlier. They are used where you may want to retrieve an existing name, address or whatever.

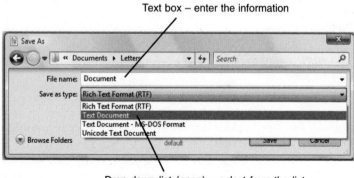

Text box – enter the information

Drop-down list (open) – select from the list

Figure 1.10 A Save As dialog box showing a text box and a drop-down list.

LISTS

With a simple list, just scroll through it and select a value. They sometimes have a linked text box. The selected value is displayed there, but you can also type in a value.

Watch your typing

When you type a value into a list's text box, e.g. to set the size of text, keep an eye on it. You often find that the application will try to complete the box by finishing the typing for you. So, you try to set the font to 7 point, and instead it is set to 72 point!

CHECKBOXES

These are switches for options – click to turn them on or off. Checkboxes are sometimes found singly, but often in sets. You can have any number of checkboxes on at the same time, unlike radio buttons.

RADIO BUTTONS

These are used to select one – and only one – from a set of alternatives. Click on the button or its name to select.

SLIDERS AND NUMBER VALUES

Sliders are used where an approximate value will do the job, for example volume

controls, speed and colour definition (actual values may not mean much to most of us in these situations!). Clicking to the side of the slider will move it towards the click point, or you can drag the slider in the direction.

Numbers are often set through scroll boxes. Click the up or down arrows to adjust the value. If you want to make a big change, type in a new value.

1.10 Turning off

When you have finished a working session, you must shut down the system properly – *do not simply turn off your PC*. Windows runs through a shutdown routine that removes any temporary files that were created by the system or by applications, checks the system and closes down safely. If you simply switch off, you may well find that it takes longer than usual to restart, as Windows will need to check – and possibly restore – essential system files.

To shut down Windows:

1 *Click the* **Start** *button, point to the arrow on the bottom right of the menu and select* **Shut Down.** *If any windows are open, they will be closed, and you may be prompted to save documents (page 35).*

Or

2 *Hold down* [**Alt**] *and press* [**F4**]. *If any windows are open, this will close the topmost one. Repeat to close all open windows, then to press* [**Alt**] + [**F4**] *again to shut down.*

ALTERNATIVE ENDINGS

If you share the PC with other people, or want to stop work for a short while, there are four options on the Shut Down menu which can end a session temporarily.

▶ **Switch User** *suspends your programs, and allows another user to log in. It doesn't matter if they use the same programs as you have been using – the documents that you were working on will not (normally) be affected by anything they do. (There may be problems if the other users try to work on documents that you have left open.) When they are finished you can log in again and pick up where you left off.*

▶ **Log Off** *shuts any open programs, but leaves the PC running, for another person to use. This is the best choice if you have finished with the PC for some time, but others will want it.*

▶ **Lock** *suspends your programs and switches to the blue-green Windows screen. To restart, you must type in your password (and there's no point in using Lock if you haven't got a password). This does not completely tie up the PC – there is a Switch User option which would allow another user to work on it. Use this to protect your work from prying eyes or careless fingers while you are away from your desk.*

▶ **Sleep** *shuts down the screen and hard drive, but leaves the memory intact. While suspended, the power consumption is virtually nil, but the computer can be restarted almost instantly. This is an attractive alternative to a full shut down if you intend to restart in less than an hour or so.*

THINGS TO REMEMBER

▶ *Windows 7 is an operating system with a package of utilities and application programs.*

▶ *The screen is referred to as the Desktop, and should be treated much as a real desktop.*

▶ *The mouse responds to single and double clicks of the left button, and to single clicks of the right button. It can also be used to drag objects across the Desktop.*

▶ *Certain keys serve specific functions.*

▶ *In any application, the commands can be reached through the menu system.*

▶ *Some commands have keyboard shortcuts.*

▶ *The Start menu gives you quick ways to start work.*

▶ *Right-clicking on an object normally opens a shortcut menu, containing relevant commands.*

▶ *Almost every object in the Wndows system has properties, which define what it looks like and how it works.*

▶ *Windows 7 has a number of simple ways to set options and make selections. At the end of a session, you can shut down, hand the PC to another user, lock it up or put it to sleep.*

SELF TEST

1 *When you click the mouse, does it matter which button you use?*

2 *What does the F1 key do?*

3 *Why doesn't your Start menu look like the one in Figure 1.3 on page 10?*

4 *What is the first key to press if you want to use the keyboard to open a menu?*

5 *What is the difference between a set of checkboxes and a set of radio buttons?*

6 *How should you end a session if someone else wants to use sthe computer after you?*

2

Programs and documents

2.1 Definitions

The whole purpose of a PC, of course, is to run applications and produce documents – almost everything in the system is concerned directly or indirectly with doing this. So, before we do anything else, let's have a look at how to run applications, and how applications and documents are interrelated. But first, some definitions.

PROGRAMS

A program is a set of instructions, that make the computer perform a task. The task may be very simple, or highly complex. It is useful to divide programs into three types:

Operating system programs are run and controlled by Windows 7 – which is itself a program (or rather a set of interlinked programs). You are only aware of them by their effect. They manage the screen, pick up your keystrokes and mouse movements, control the transfer of data to and from the disk drives, prepare documents for output to the printer, and similar chores. Those of us who cut our computing teeth on older operating systems sometimes regret that Windows takes such total control of these, but overall, Windows does a good job of management.

Utilities are the programs that you can use to manage your PC. Windows Explorer, for example, allows you to organize your file storage (Chapter 7). There are programs in the Control Panel (Chapter 10) which you can use to customize the hardware and software, and another set that enable you to keep your disks in good order (Chapter 13).

Applications are why you use computers. They include business applications such as word processors, spreadsheets, databases and accounts packages; graphics software for creating and editing images; browsers and other tools for communicating and working on the Internet and on local networks; multimedia viewers, players and editing software; games and much else. Most, though not all, applications will produce or display documents, and any given application can only handle documents of a certain type or range of types. We'll return to this in a moment.

DOCUMENTS

In Windows jargon, a *document* is an organized set of information produced by an application. It can be stored on disk as a file and – typically but not always – can be output onto paper, to be read or viewed away from the computer. The most obvious examples of documents are letters, essays and reports created on word processors, but databases, spreadsheets and Web pages are also documents, as are images, sound and video files. When a document is saved, part of its name identifies the application that created it. This association with applications is central to the way that Windows handles documents. We will return to it in section 7.9.

2.2 Start > All Programs

When we looked briefly at the Start menu in Chapter 1, we noted that the programs you use most often are listed in it. In fact, all of the programs already on your PC, and any that you install later, should have an entry here, under the **All Programs** heading. A program may be listed as an item on the main menu, or may have been grouped into a folder – which may itself have a further level of folders. These Start menu entries and folders are created by the routines that install Windows 7 and later applications. If you do not like the structure, you can tailor it to suit yourself (see Chapter 11).

What's > this?

In this book, > is used to link the steps in a menu sequence, e.g. **Start > All Programs > Accessories > Paint** means 'select **Start,** from its menu pick **All Programs** then pick **Accessories** and finally select **Paint**'.

To start a program:
1 *Click the* **Start** *button or press the window key on your keyboard.*
2 *Click on* **All Programs.**
3 *If necessary, click on a folder name to open it up – repeat as needed until you can see the program name.*
4 *Click on a program name.*
▶ *If the Start menu has got very crowded, or there are lots of entries in a folder, you may need to use the scroll bar to see the entry you want.*

2.3 Start Search

Beneath the programs area of the Start menu is a box labelled 'Start Search'. If you type part or all of the name of a program or document, Windows will search through the Start menu – and then on through the rest of the system – to find matching files. Note that it doesn't just search through the names, but also the content of files and this can produce some random results. However, it does find all matching programs very efficiently, and these are listed at the top of the display.

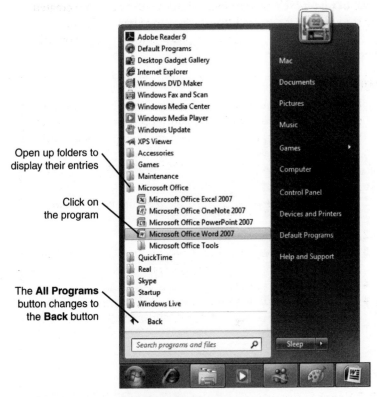

Open up folders to display their entries

Click on the program

The **All Programs** button changes to the **Back** button

Figure 2.1 Starting from the All Programs *area of the Start menu.*

1 *Click the* **Start** *button or press the* **Windows** *key on your keyboard.*

2 *Type the first few letters of the program name into the Start Search area – do not press* **[Enter]**. *Windows will start to match and list the possible programs as soon as you have typed the first letter. If you press* **[Enter]** *at any point, this will start whichever program is at the top of the list.*

3 *The programs display on the left of the menu will be replaced by a list of matching programs, documents and files.*

4 *Click on the program that you want, or move the highlight to it with the arrow keys and press* [**Enter**]*.*

Matching programs
are listed at the top

Those documents
that match best are
listed here

There may be lots
more matches –
click here to see
them all

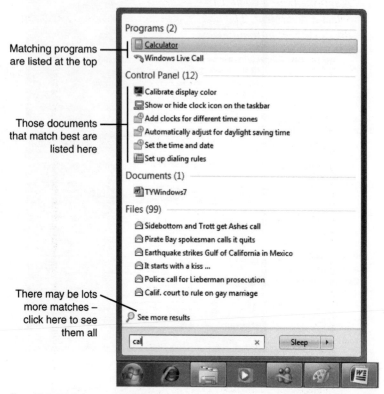

Figure 2.2 Starting from a search. The See all results item will show you everything that matched – and almost all of it will be irrelevant, as the likely matches have been selected for display.

2.4 Starting from documents

Every type of document is – or can be – linked to an application (see page 136), so that when you open a document, Windows will run the appropriate application for you. The Start menu has links to those folders where you probably store many of your files – *Documents*, *Pictures* and *Music* – and it also lists the files that you have been working on recently in submenus that open from the programs that are displayed on the menu.

1 *Click on* **Start**.
2 *Point to a program that has a black arrowhead to its right. A sub-menu will open listing recently-used files.*
3 *Select a document. The linked application will start, opening the document automatically.*

Figure 2.3 Selecting a recently used document from its program's link on the Start menu.

2.5 Starting from Windows Explorer

Windows Explorer is the built-in file management application. You have almost certainly been using it already, though you may not have been aware of that. When you click the Documents, Pictures or other links on the right of the Start menu, it opens the named folder in Windows Explorer, though it doesn't actually say 'Windows Explorer' on the screen. We will be looking closely at this vital application in Chapter 7, but at this point it is worth noting that programs can be started from within it.

Running a program this way can be tricky – simply locating it can take time. So why would you want to do this? Well, sometimes you have to. For example, if you download software from the Web, it is often in the form of a self-extracting Zip file – compressed and stored in a program. When this is run, it installs the software onto your PC. That initial downloaded file will not have a menu entry. To run it, you have to find it on your disk and run it through Windows Explorer. And if you haven't changed the default settings, it will be stored in the Downloads folder. Here is what you would do.

1 *Open the Start menu and click on the* **Computer** *button. This will start Windows Explorer and display the main folders on your computer.*

Figure 2.4 Programs can be run from Windows Explorer, and have to be if they are not yet installed in your computer and added to the Start menu.

2 *Click* **Downloads** *at the top of the section on the left to display the contents of the Downloads folder in the area on the right.*

3 *Double-click on the program name to start it.*

Installing is easy

Installing new software on your computer is normally very, very simple. Almost all modern applications are supplied with installation routines that do all the tricky stuff for you as you see when you get the Live Essentials package.

TASKBAR BUTTONS

When a program is running, it has a matching button on the Taskbar, but you will have noticed that there are some buttons which are always there – for Internet Explorer, Windows Explorer and Media Player. These offer a quick way to start the program – just click on the button. You can pin more buttons to the Taskbar if you like this way of starting applications.

1 *Run the program (from the Start menu) that you want to add to the permanent set of buttons.*

2 *Right-click on the button.*

3 *Select* **Pin this program to Taskbar.**

That's it. Next time you turn on your PC, there will be a button on the Taskbar for that program. Click on the button to start it.

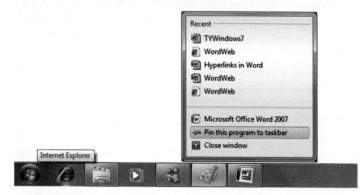

Figure 2.5 Pinning a program to the Taskbar gives you a quick way to start it.

DESKTOP SHORTCUTS

Shortcuts offer a quick route to regularly-used folders and programs. When you first start using Windows 7, you will find a few of these icons on the Desktop, leading to programs or folders. Click on a shortcut to run the program, or to open the folder.

There are half a dozen standard shortcuts that you can add or remove, as you like (see page 93), and you can create and add your own shortcuts to favourite folders and applications. This can be done easily through Windows Explorer (see page 123).

A tidy desktop?

Some people love shortcuts and cover their Desktops with them. I prefer to only have shortcuts to those few things that I like to keep close at hand. This is not because I'm a tidy person – I'm not – but if there are more than a dozen or so shortcuts on the Desktop, it can take a little while to find the one you want.

2.6 Filenames and extensions

When documents are saved onto disk, they are given a name which has two parts. The first part identifies that particular document, and can be more or less anything you want (see *Rules for filenames*, below). The second part is a three-letter extension which identifies the type of document. This is normally set by the application in which the document is created, and it is through this extension that Windows can link documents and applications. (We'll look at how to create these links on page 136.)

Here are some extensions that you are likely to meet:

- ▶ *txt*   *Simple text, without any formatting or styling*
- ▶ *docx*   *Word 2007 document*
- ▶ *doc*   *older Word document*
- ▶ *htm*   *Web page – can be created by many applications*
- ▶ *bmp*   *bitmap image, e.g. from Paint*
- ▶ *gif*   *a standard format for images on Web pages*
- ▶ *jpg*   *an alternative format for Web page images*
- ▶ *exe*   *an executable program – not a document*
- ▶ *zip*   *a file containing one or more files that have been compressed to save disk space.*

Invisible extensions

By default, Windows Explorer does not show the extensions of files, but the icon beside a filename will either show what type of file it is or give a thumbnail picture of it, or show a program's logo.

RULES FOR FILENAMES

The first part of the name can be any length (up to 250 characters!) and can consist of letters, numbers, spaces and underlines, but no other symbols. It's good sense to make sure that the name means something to you, so that you can identify the file when you come back to it later – and the shorter the name, the smaller the chance of making a mistake if you have to type it again.

STANDARD FORMATS

Life would be easier if there was only one standard format for each type of document, but instead there are loads of them, especially for word-processing and graphics. You might wonder why. According to the old joke, computer people love standards – which is why they have so many. In fact, there are several reasons. When a software house develops a new application, or a new version of an existing one, it will sometimes use a different document format – partly to handle its special features, and partly to distinguish it from its rivals. Some formats are developed to meet particular needs. With graphics documents, for instance, there is a trade-off between file size and image quality, and formats have been developed across the range.

The extension must match the application. As a general rule, when you save a file for the first time, simply give the identifying name and let the application set the extension. If the application can output documents in different formats, and you know that you need a particular format, select it from the **Save as type** list. After the first save, the filename is set, though the file could be later saved under a different name and in a different format. You might, for example, have edited a Word document to make it into a Web page, and so need to save it as an HTML file.

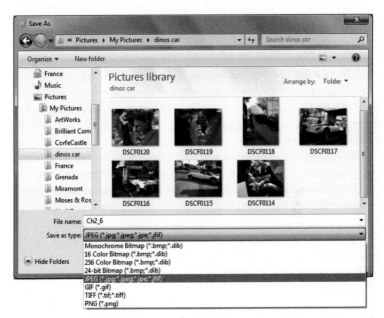

Figure 2.6 A typical Save As dialog box. This one is from Paint which can save in several formats. All programs have their native format, and many can import or export files in other formats for transfer between programs.

2.7 Closing programs

When you have finished using an application, it must be closed down properly. Closing its window will close the program, but you will also find a **Close** or **Exit** option on the **File** menu. The key combination **[Alt] + [F4]** also closes applications.

File	Edit	Format	View	Help
New			Ctrl+N	
Open...			Ctrl+O	
Save			Ctrl+S	
Save As...				
Page Setup...				
Print...			Ctrl+P	
Exit				

If you have created or edited a file, and not saved the changes, you will be prompted to save before the application closes.

- *Select **Save** (or **Yes** – they vary) to save.*
- *Select **Don't Save** (or **No**) to exit without saving.*
- *Select **Cancel** to return to the application.*

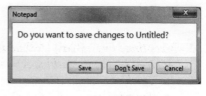

The double-check

Whenever you do anything which could be potentially dangerous to the system, Windows will ask you to confirm. This is a safety feature. It is there in case a rogue program got into your PC and tried to change the settings or delete files.

2.8 Coping with crashes

Windows 7 is more reliable and robust than earlier versions of Windows, but software is rarely perfect. Some applications – and some combinations of applications – are more likely than others to crash. If you are interested, crashes are normally caused by two programs trying to use the same area of memory, and you can go find a big technical book if you want to know more! If you are lucky, you won't have crashes often. But just in case...

If you see any of these, your PC has probably crashed.

- *The busy symbol appears and stays (but wait twice as long as normal just in case it has more to do than you thought).*
- *No response to key presses or mouse actions.*
- *The screen does not display properly – there might be part of a window or dialog box left behind and unmovable.*

This will often solve the problem:

1 *Press these keys: [Ctrl] [Alt] and [Delete]. The Desktop will be replaced by the green-blue screen, with the options:*
   ▷ *Lock this computer*
   ▷ *Switch User*
   ▷ *Log off*
   ▷ *Change a password*
   ▷ *Start Task Manager.*
2 *Click* Start Task Manager. *The* Task Manager *dialog box will appear. Open the* Applications *tab if it is not already open. The program that has crashed should be at the top of the list – with 'Not responding' after the name.*
3 *If an application is not responding, click* End Task *– and confirm when prompted. The system should work properly once it is out of the way.*
4 *If the highlighted program is not marked 'Not responding', it probably hasn't crashed – click* ▨ *to close Task Manager and give Windows a bit longer to sort itself out.*

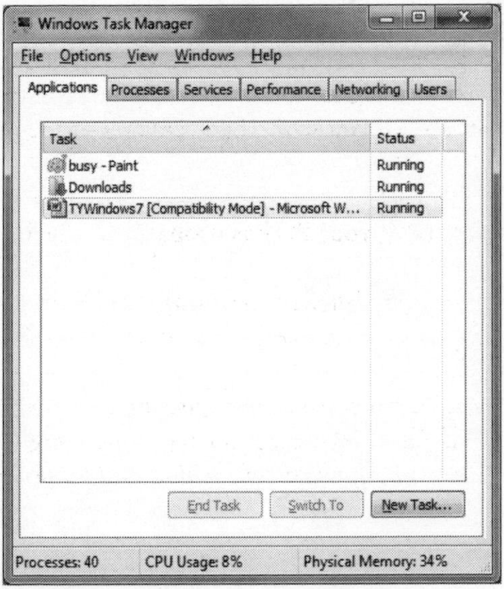

Figure 2.7 The Task Manager dialog box open at the Applications *tab.*

Find the switch

If Task Manager cannot handle the crash – and this will arise every now and then – there is normally a 'Restart' button somewhere on the front of a PC's case. Press this to restart the PC – when it's running again, the problem will have disappeared. If you cannot find a Restart button, holding the normal Start button in for 5 seconds or so will usually make the machine restart. If all else fails, switch the PC off at the wall, wait 10 seconds and switch it back on again. (This won't work with battery-powered laptops, but holding the Start button down usually works with those.)

THINGS TO REMEMBER

▶ *There are three main types of programs: operating system, utilities and applications.*

▶ *The data files produced by or displayed by applications are called documents.*

▶ *Programs can be started from the Start menu, the Taskbar or from within Windows Explorer.*

▶ *Opening a document will run its associated application.*

▶ *Programs should be closed down properly when you have finished using them.*

▶ *Filenames have two parts: an identifying name and an extension which describes the format of the file.*

▶ *If a program crashes, the* [Ctrl] + [Alt] + [Delete] *key combination will take you to a screen where you can open the Task Manager dialog box.*

SELF TEST

1 *Is Windows 7 an operating system or an application?*

2 *In Windows jargon, what is a 'document'?*

3 *What is the quickest way to start a program?*

4 *What happens if you try to close a program without saving the work you have done on a document?*

5 *In a filename, what does the extension do?*

6 *When might you want to use Task Manager?*

3

Working with windows

3.1 Basic windows concepts

A window is a framed area of the screen that exists and is controlled independently of any other windows. All applications are displayed in windows. If an application can handle multiple documents, they may each be displayed in their own window within the application.

If you only use one application at a time, you don't have to think too much about managing your windows – there will only be the one. But this kind of usage does not take advantage of Windows 7, which is a multi-tasking system. If you are going to have several applications open at once, you must know how to switch between them, and how to arrange their windows so that you can work efficiently. This chapter will show you how.

A window normally has these features:

▶ A **Title bar** *showing the name of the application and the current document;*
▶ **Minimize, Maximize** *and* **Close** *buttons on the far right of the title bar – for changing the mode (page 43) and for shutting down;*
▶ *An icon at the far left of the Title Bar – leading to the window's* **Control menu** *(page 43);*
▶ *Or in newer Microsoft programs; a button which opens the menu of document-level commands.*

▶ **Scroll bars** *along the right and bottom – for moving the contents within the frame. These are only present if the contents are too wide or too long to fit within the frame.*

▶ *A thin outer* **border** *– for changing the window size (page 50).*

Application windows also have:

▶ **Menu bar** *– leading to the full set of commands and options;*

▶ *One or more* **toolbars** *– containing icons that call up the more commonly-used commands and options. Toolbars are normally along the top of the working area, but may be down either side, or as 'floating' panels anywhere on screen.*

▶ *In newer Microsoft programs the commands may be presented on a* **Ribbon** *of tools instead of, or as well as the menu bar and toolbars.*

▶ *The* **Status bar** *– displaying a variety of information about the current activity in the application.*

Figure 3.1 The main features of windows.

SCREEN MODES

Both application and document windows can be in one of three modes, and the simplest way to switch them is with the buttons at the top right:

 Minimize – An application is then visible only as a button on the Taskbar. A minimized document is reduced so that only the Title bar and window control buttons are visible.

 Maximize – An application window fills the screen and loses its outer frame. When a document is maximized in its application's working area, its Title bar is merged with the application Title bar and its window control buttons are placed on the far right of the Menu bar.

 Restore – The window is smaller than the full screen or working area. Its size can be adjusted, and it can be moved to any position – within or beyond the limits of the screen.

Restore is on the **Maximize** button in a maximized window, and on the **Minimize** button of a minimized window.

THE CONTROL MENU

This can be opened by clicking the icon at the far left of the Title bar. But this is really here for keyboard users.

1 *Press* [**Alt**] *and the* [**Space bar**] *to open the menu.*
2 *You can now Mi**n**imize, Ma**x**imize/**R**estore or **C**lose by pressing the keys of the underlined letters. (*[**Alt**] + [**F4**] *is a shortcut for* **Close***.)*

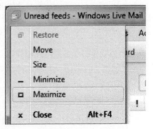

3 *This is also where keyboard users start to **M**ove (page 53) or change the **S**ize (page 51) of the window.*

3.2 Using the scroll bars

When you are working on a large picture or a long document, only the part that you are working on will be displayed within the window. Scroll bars will be present along the bottom and/or right of the frame and can be used to move the hidden parts of the document into the working area. They can be controlled in three ways:

▶ *Click on the arrows at the ends to nudge the contents in the direction of the arrow – typically the movement will be a line or so at a time, but the amount of movement varies with the application and document size.*

▶ *Click on the bar to the side of or above or below the slider for a larger movement – typically just less than the height or width of the working area.*

▶ *Drag the slider. This is the quickest way to scroll through a large document.*

Automatic scrolling

If the typing, drawing or other movements that you make while working on your document take the current position out of the visible area, the document will be scrolled automatically to bring the current position back into view.

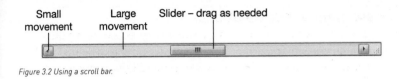

Figure 3.2 Using a scroll bar.

3.3 Screen layouts

Windows 7 allows you enormous flexibility in your layouts, though
the simplest that will do the job is usually the best. You can only
ever work on one application at a time – but that is a limitation
of humans, not computers. However, you can copy or move
files or data between two windows and there may be continuing
activities, such as printing or downloading, going on in other
windows. If you do not actually need to see what is happening in
the other windows, the simplest layout is to run all applications
in Maximized mode. The one that you are working on will fill the
screen, obscuring the others, but you can easily bring one of those
to the front by clicking on its button in the Taskbar.

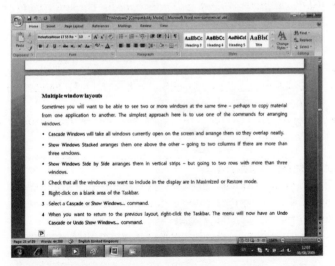

Figure 3.3 If you are only working on one application, you may as well run it in a Maximized window and have
the largest working/viewing area. Other windows can be reached, when needed, through their Taskbar buttons.

MULTIPLE WINDOW LAYOUTS

Sometimes you will want to be able to see two or more windows at the same time – perhaps to copy material from one application to another. The simplest approach here is to use one of the commands for arranging windows. They affect only those windows which are currently open on the screen – not those that have been minimized to the Taskbar.

▶ **Cascade Windows** *will take all open windows and arrange them so they overlap neatly.*

▶ **Show Windows Stacked** *arranges them one above the other – going to two columns if there are more than three windows.*

▶ **Show Windows Side by Side** *arranges them in vertical strips – but going to two rows with more than three windows.*

1 *Check that all the windows you want to include in the display are in Maximized or Restore mode.*
2 *Right-click on a blank area of the Taskbar.*
3 *Select a* **Cascade** *or* **Show Windows…** *command.*
4 *When you want to return to the previous layout, right-click the Taskbar. The menu will now have an* **Undo Cascade** *or* **Undo Show Windows…** *command.*

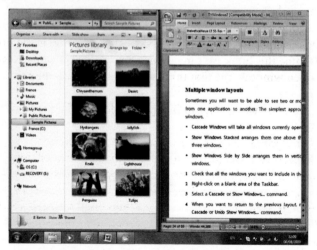

Figure 3.4 The Stacked or Side by Side displays work better with bigger screens. An 1024 × 768 screen can cope with two windows – more at a pinch.

Figure 3.5 The Taskbar's shortcut menu with its window display options.

It's your Desktop...

... and you can arrange windows exactly how you like. Individual windows can be resized and moved (read on to find out how), and the stacked and cascade layouts aren't fixed, but can be treated as a start point to get the arrangement you want.

3.4 Switching between windows

You can only work in the active window – the topmost one. And if you've got a pile-up and can't quite work out which one is on top, the Close button in the top right of the active window is red not grey (shame this book isn't in colour). So, when you want to work in an open window, the first thing to do is bring it to the top.

There are two simple ways to bring a window to the top:

▶ *If you can see any part of the window, click on it.*
▶ *Point to its Taskbar button – a thumbnail image of the window will appear. If there are multiple copies of the program running, e.g. if you have two Word documents open at once, then there will be a thumbnail for each window. Point to a thumbnail to bring its window to the front for a better look, or click on the thumbnail to switch to that window.*

Figure 3.6 Using the Taskbar to switch between windows.

TABBING TO WINDOWS

Sometimes you cannot see the window you want to reach, and switching between windows by using their Taskbar buttons is not always convenient. Here is a neat alternative:

1 *Hold down* [**Alt**] *and press* [**Tab**]. *This panel appears.*
2 *Press* [**Tab**] *again until the application that you want is highlighted – if you go off the end, it cycles back to the start.*
3 *Release* [**Alt**]. *The selected window will come to the front.*

FLIP 3D

This displays all open windows – including those minimized onto the Taskbar – sideways on and reduced in size, but clear enough to be able to see what is happening. You can cycle through them, bringing each to the front in turn, where it is larger and easier to see, until you find the one you want.

1 *Hold down the* [Windows] *key and press* [Tab].
2 *Repeat Step 1. The windows will cycle round from left to right, with the one at the front going to the back of the queue.*
3 *When the one you want is at the front, release* [Windows].

Figure 3.7 Using Flip 3D to switch to another window.

Keep life simple

In computer use, as elsewhere in life, simpler is generally better. Unless you particularly like Flip 3D, use the Taskbar for switching between windows, or [Alt] + [Tab] if you use the keyboard instead of the mouse.

3.5 Adjusting the window size

When a window is in Restore mode, its size can be adjusted freely. This can be done easily with the mouse or – less easily – with the keyboard.

USING THE MOUSE

1 *Select the document or application window.*
2 *Point to an edge or corner of the frame – when you are in a suitable place the cursor changes to a double-headed arrow.*
3 *Hold down the left button and drag an edge or a corner to change the window size.*
4 *Release the mouse button.*
5 *Repeat on other edges or corners if necessary.*

Figure 3.8 Adjusting the size of a window. It can be more efficient to change the size by dragging a corner, rather than an edge, but it is trickier to locate the cursor at the start.

1 *Open the Control menu. Hold down* [Alt] *and press the* [Space bar].

2 *Press S to select Size.*
3 *Press the arrow key corresponding to the edge that you want to move. A double-headed arrow will appear on that edge.*
4 *Use the arrow keys to move the edge into its new position.*
5 *Press* [Enter] *to fix the new size.*
6 *Repeat for the other edges or corners if necessary.*

3.6 Moving windows

A window in Restore mode can be moved to anywhere on – or part-ways off – the screen. The Title bar is the 'handle' for movement. In those applications that display documents in their own windows, these windows can be moved around the working area of the application in exactly the same way.

MOVING WITH THE MOUSE

▶ *Point to anywhere on the Title bar and drag the window to its new place.*

MOVING WITH THE KEYBOARD

1 *Open the Control menu and select* **Move.**
2 *Use the arrow keys to move the window as required.*
3 *Press* **[Enter]** *to fix the new position.*

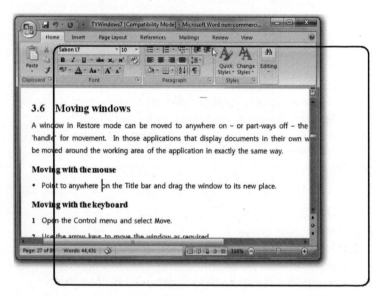

Figure 3.9 Moving a window by dragging on the Title bar.

3.7 Closing windows

When you have finished with a window, close it.

There are three methods which will work with any window:

▶ *Click the* **Close** *button*  *in the top right corner.*

▶ *Hold down* [**Alt**] *and press* [**Space bar**] *to open the Control menu and select* **Close**.

▶ *Hold down the* [**Alt**] *key and press* [**F4**].

EXIT AND CLOSE

You can also close a window by exiting from an application (see section 2.7, *Closing programs*, page 35).

Declutter!
Get into the habit of closing windows when you have finished with them. This will free up memory so that other applications run more smoothly, as well as reducing the clutter on your Desktop.

THINGS TO REMEMBER

▶ *Windows can be open in Maximized, Restore or Minimized mode.*

▶ *To switch between the display modes, use the control buttons on the top right of the frame, or the commands on the Control menu.*

▶ *If the contents of a window go beyond the boundaries of the frame, the scroll bars can be used to pull distant areas into view.*

▶ *There are many different ways to arrange windows on your screen – the simplest is to work with all windows Maximized, pulling them to the front as needed.*

▶ *The Cascade and Show Windows arrangements will display (part of) all the windows in Maximized and Restore mode.*

▶ *You can switch between open windows by holding down [Alt] and pressing [Tab].*

▶ *You can flip through graphics of each window by holding down [Windows] and pressing [Tab].*

▶ *The size of a window can be changed by dragging on an edge or corner, or using the Control menu Size command and the arrow keys.*

▶ *Windows can be moved by dragging on their Title bar, or with the Control menu Move command.*

▶ *Windows should be closed when no longer needed to reduce screen clutter and free up memory.*

SELF TEST

1 *What are the three possible screen modes for a window? How do you change modes?*

2 *Where will you find the Cascade Windows command?*

3 *How can you use the [Tab] key to switch between windows?*

4 *If you want to drag a window across the screen, how do you get hold of it?*

5 *What happens when you close a window? How do you do it?*

4

....

Basic skills

4.1 Selection techniques

Before you can do any work on an object or a set of objects –
e.g. format a block of text, copy part of an image, move a group
of files from one folder to another – you must first select it.

TEXT

Use WordPad or any word processor to try out these techniques.
They can also be used with text objects in graphics packages and
even with small items of text such as filenames.

With the mouse:

1 *Point to the start of the text.*
2 *Hold down the left mouse button and drag across the screen.*
3 *The selected text will be highlighted.*

With the keyboard:

1 *Move the cursor to the start of the text.*
2 *Hold down* [Shift].
3 *Use the arrow keys to highlight the text you want.*

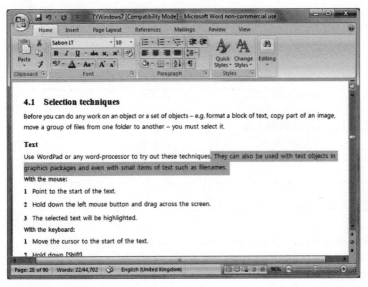

Figure 4.1 Once text has been selected, it can be edited, copied, moved, deleted or formatted.

Keys give more control

If you want to select several pages of text in Word, or on a long Web page, it is usually better to do it with the [Shift] key and arrows. If you use the mouse, the pages may well scroll away beneath you, faster than you can control them.

GRAPHICS

The same techniques are used for images in graphics applications, and for icons on the Desktop, files in Computer and other screen objects.

Single object:

▶ *Point to it. If this does not highlight the object, click on it.*

Adjacent objects:

1 *Imagine a rectangle that will enclose the objects.*
2 *Point to one corner of this rectangle.*

3 *Hold down the left mouse button and drag across to the opposite corner – an outline will appear as you do this.*

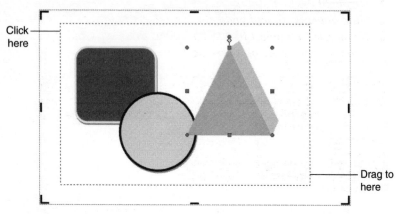

Figure 4.2 Selecting drawn objects. Point to one corner then drag to the opposite corner.

Or where the objects are in a set, e.g. the icons and files

4 *Select the object at one corner.*
5 *Hold down* **[Shift]** *and click on the object at the opposite corner.*

Figure 4.3 Selecting a continuous group of icons in Explorer. Select the first object then hold [Shift] and select the last.

Scattered objects:

1 *Highlight the first object.*
2 *Hold down* [**Ctrl**] *and highlight each object in turn.*
3 *If you select an object by mistake, point to (or click on) it again to remove the highlighting.*

Figure 4.4 Selecting a scattered set of icons in Explorer. Select the first object then hold [Ctrl] and select the others.

4.2 Cut, Copy and Paste

If you look at the Clipboard group of any newer Windows application, or the Edit menu of an older one, you will find the commands **Cut, Copy** and **Paste**. You will also find them on the short menu that opens when you right-click on a selected object. These are used for copying and moving data within and between applications.

► **Copy** *copies a selected block of text, picture, file or other object into a special part of memory called the* Clipboard. *Data stored in the Clipboard can be retrieved by any Windows application – not just the one that put it there.*

► **Cut** *deletes selected data from the original application, but places a copy into the Clipboard.*

► **Paste** *copies the data from the Clipboard into a different place in the same application, or into a different application – as long as this can handle data in that format.*

The data normally remains in the Clipboard until new data is copied or cut into it, or until Windows is shut down. (Some applications have a **Clear Clipboard** command.)

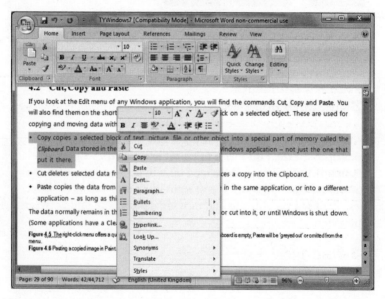

Figure 4.5 The right-click menu offers a quick route to the Cut and Paste commands. If the Clipboard is empty, Paste will be 'greyed out' or omitted from the menu.

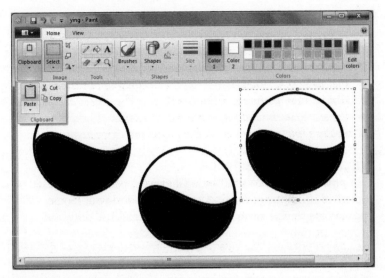

Figure 4.6 Pasting a copied image in Paint.

Keyboard shortcuts

These keyboard shortcuts work in all Windows applications. Learn them – it will save you so much time!

Cut [Ctrl] + [X]
Copy [Ctrl] + [C]
Paste [Ctrl] + [V]

4.3 Drag and drop

This is an alternative to Cut and Paste for moving objects within an application or between compatible applications. It is also the simplest way to rearrange files and folders, as you will see in Chapter 7.

The technique is simple to explain:

1 *Select the block of text or the object(s).*
2 *Point anywhere within the highlighted text or in the frame enclosing other objects.*
3 *Hold down the mouse button and drag the object across the screen or, with text, move the cursor (which is now ☝).*
4 *Release the button to drop the object into its new position.*

Practice makes perfect

In practice, accurate positioning depends upon good mouse control. And one of the best ways to improve your mouse control is to play the games. The card games use drag-and-drop for moving cards; Minesweeper helps to build speed and accuracy. (Remember this when you need an excuse.)

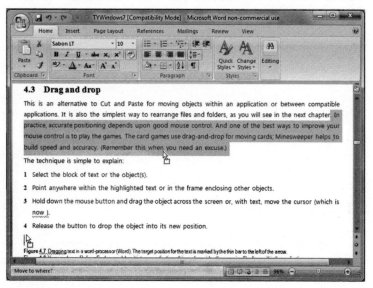

Figure 4.7 Dragging text in a word processor (Word). The target position for the text is marked by the thin bar to the left of the arrow.

Figure 4.8 You can drag a file from Explorer and drop it into an application – this can be quicker than opening files from within the application.

THINGS TO REMEMBER

▶ *Text can be selected with the mouse or the keyboard.*

▶ *Graphics and other objects are selected by dragging an outline around them, or by using the mouse in conjunction with [Shift] or [Ctrl].*

▶ *Selected data can be cut or copied to the Clipboard, then pasted into the same or a different application.*

▶ *Text and some objects can be moved by drag and drop.*

SELF TEST

1 *When selecting text or objects, how can the [Shift] key help?*

2 *When would you use [Ctrl] while selecting objects?*

3 *What is the Clipboard?*

4 *How can you open a document using drag and drop?*

5

....

Help!

5.1 Help and Support

If you ever get stuck while using Windows, there's plenty of help at hand. Windows 7 has its own extensive Help and Support system with 'tours', 'tutorials' and interactive troubleshooters, and every Windows application has a Help system.

The main Windows 7 Help system is reached through the **Help and Support** item on the **Start** menu.

▶ *Click* **Start,** *select* **Help and Support** *and you are in.*

There are basically three ways to get help.

▶ **Search for it, by typing in some words to describe what you want to know.** *This is more useful after you have been using Windows for a while and understand more of the jargon and more about how things work.*
▶ *Follow a link. On the top page there are three:*
   ▷ *How to get started with your computer*
   ▷ *Learn about Windows basics*
   ▷ *Browse Help topics*
▶ *Go to the Windows website*

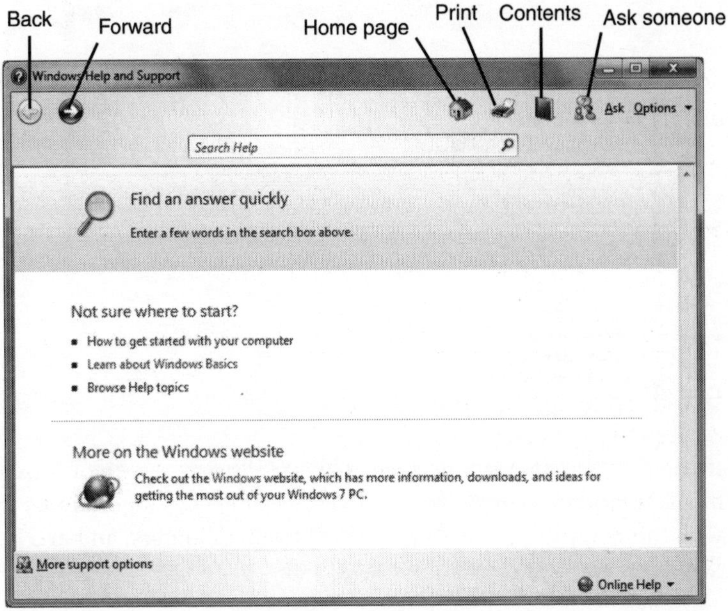

Back Forward   Home page Print Contents Ask someone

Figure 5.1 The Home page of the Help and Support system – the buttons at the top give quick access to the main tools, and notice the Search field.

HOW TO GET STARTED WITH YOUR COMPUTER

This is written for people who have previously used another computer. There's advice here about transferring files across from the old machine, setting up the Internet connection and things like that.

WINDOWS BASICS

This leads to a set of links, each leading to an article on a basic concept and/or technique. Within the articles you will then find other links taking you off to explore ideas in more detail, or demonstrating how things work.

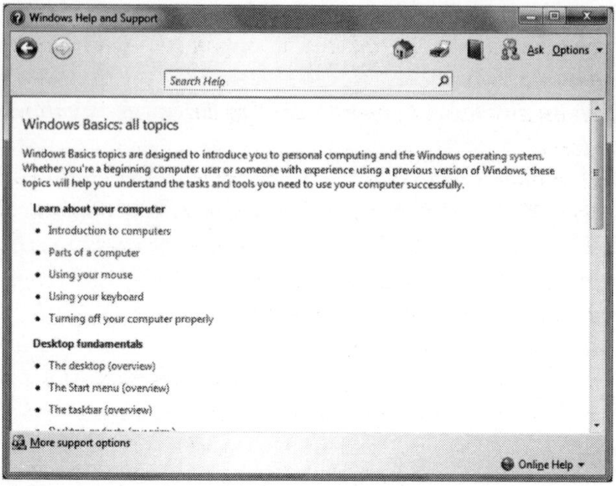

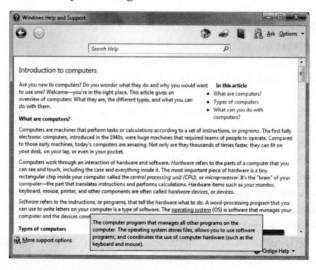

Figure 5.2 The Windows Basics area of the Help system – if you are new to Windows, you should at least dip into here early on.

1 *Click the text for Windows Basics.*
2 *Click on a topic heading.*

Figure 5.3 If text is in green clicking on it displays a tip. Notice 'Show all' at the top right – click this to display any hidden details anywhere in the article. (See also step 7.)

3 *The article will be displayed. Read it straight through, or...*
4 *Click a link in the 'In this article' set on the right to jump down to a subtopic.*
5 *Click on any text in green to display a brief explanation of the term.*
6 *Text in blue is usually a link to another article in the Help system. If the text has an arrow at the start, it tells you that clicking on the text will start a program, or open a dialog box, or do something similar. The Help article will stay open, so that you can read through its instructions while you try out the program, or whatever.*
7 *If you see blue text with an arrowhead to its left, this indicates there is more detail available under the header text. Click anywhere on the text to show the details.*
8 *When you have finished with an article, click the Back button to go back to the previous page – you may need to click it several times to reach the Home page again.*

5.2 Browse Help topics

This gives you access to the entire offline (built-in) Help system. It is arranged into 16 main areas, which are subdivided into subtopics – which may also be subdivided.

1 *Click the 'Browse Help topics' text, or click the toolbar button.*
2 *A solid blue block beside a heading tell you that this leads to the next level down. Click on the heading to see a list of articles and headings for subtopics.*
3 *A page icon beside a heading tells you that this leads to an article. Click to read it.*
4 *Read, and follow up links until you find what you need. If you want to go back, click the Back button or click a heading in the list of topics through which you have browsed to reach this page.*

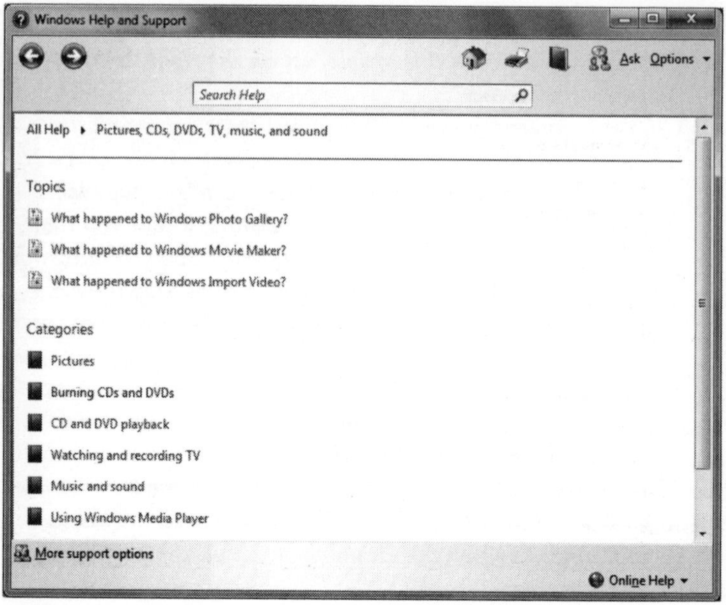

Figure 5.4 Browsing through the Contents. Note the list of topic headings at the top. These show the route you have taken to reach this page – click on any of these to jump back to that point in the system.

5.3 Search

The **Search** box is present in the toolbar on every page of the Help system. To run a search:

1 *Type one or more keywords into the box and press Enter or click* 🔍*.*
2 *The 'best' 25 results, i.e. those which Windows calculates will best match your search, will be listed. Click on a heading to display the page.*
3 *If you don't find what you want, try different keywords. Sometimes it is better not to be too specific.*

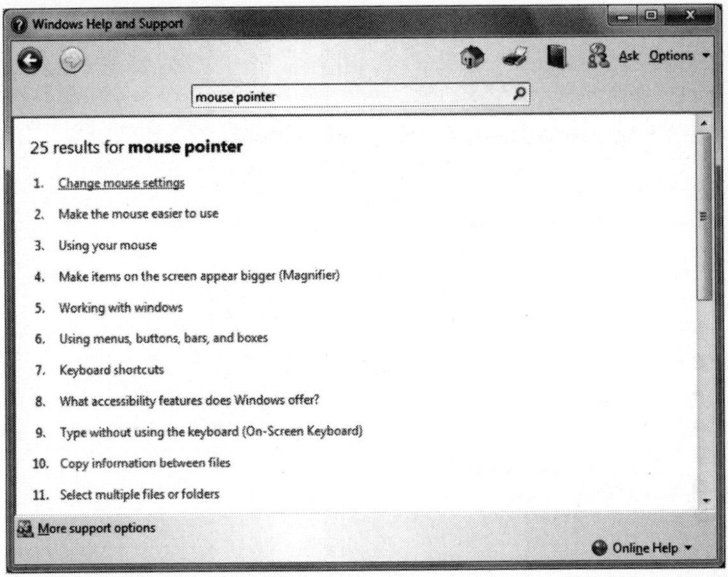

Figure 5.5 Searching for Help. If Online Help is switched on (see page 74), the routine will search the online Help system at Microsoft as well as the pages in your PC.

Keywords

When searching in the newsgroups, or in the main Help system, a 'keyword' is simply a word that describes what you are looking for. If a word does not give you what you want, try a different word.

5.4 Help with hardware problems

When you are looking for Help with a hardware problem, you may well meet a troubleshooter. These can be very useful, especially when you are having difficulties with printers or other peripherals, or when you are trying to configure your Internet and e-mail software. They will normally take you through a series of checks to diagnose problems and can often tell you what to do to cure them.

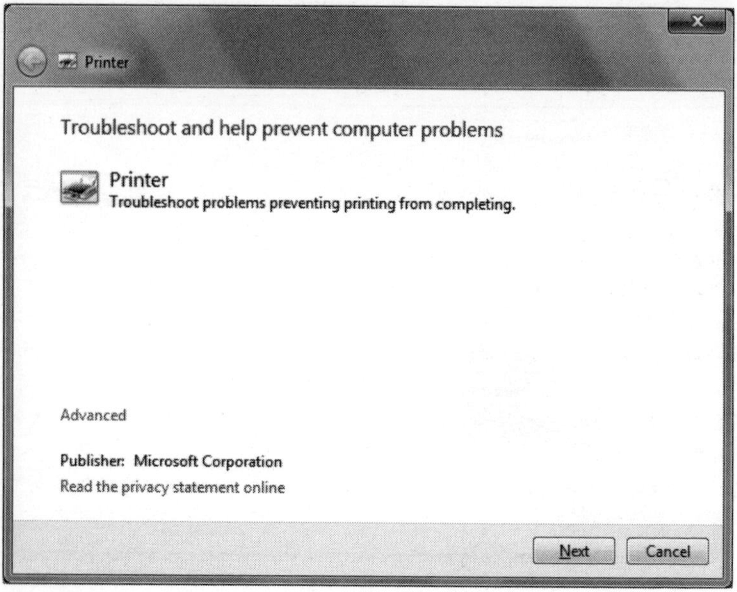

Figure 5.6 The Printer Troubleshooter starting work – it does most of the hard work for you!

With other problems, the Help article may ask to run a system tool, such as Device Manager, and take you through a series of steps to check settings and correct them if necessary.

5.5 The Windows website

The Windows website is an excellent source of additional Help, in the form of articles and videos, plus access to a forum where you can post questions and (hopefully) get replies from Microsoft's experts or from other users who have met and solved the same problems.

1 *Click the Windows website link on the home page of the Help system.*

Figure 5.7 There's lots more Help at the Windows website.

2 *Click on a topic heading to read an article or watch a video, or*
3 *Click 'Ask the community' to go to the forum.*
4 *Click on a question's heading to read it and its replies, or*
5 *Type one or more words into the Search forums box to describe what you are looking for, then click the magnifying glass icon to start the search.*

Figure 5.8 Browsing for help in the Windows forum. If you want to ask questions, you must join – it's free and painless to do so!

Online Help

When you search for Help, the search can be just within the core material stored in your PC, or also in the store of more specialized and constantly updated Help online at Microsoft. By default, a search will include the online Help, but if you have a slow Internet connection, or are not connected at all, this is not useful.

To change the setting:

1 *Click the* **Offline Help** *(or* **Online Help***) button.*
2 *Select* **Get online/offline Help** *to change the setting for the current session.*

Or

3 *Select* **Settings.**
4 *Tick (or clear) the* **Include Windows Online...** *option.*
5 *Click* **OK.**

Figure 5.9 This setting controls how the Help system normally works – you can override it during a session if you need to go online (or stay off).

Search in applications

Many Windows programs have a Search box in the toolbar.
Use this to find Help for that program.

5.6 Help tools and options

On the right of the toolbar there are five buttons:

▶ **Home** *takes you back to the page you see when you first open Help and Support.*
▶ **Print...** *prints the current article.*
▶ **Browse Help** *takes you to the Table of Contents.*
▶ **Ask** *opens a page with links to get Help online. You can use* **Remote Assistance** *to link your PC to a friend's so that you can see each other's screens and try to sort out the problem between you. You can also access the newsgroup* **communities,** *contact Customer Support online, search through the databases online, or phone Customer Services.*
▶ **Options** *repeats two of these tools, and gives you three more. Let's have a closer look at this.*

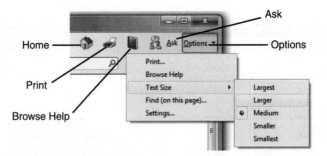

Figure 5.10 The Help tools and options.

Options
There are five options:

▶ **Print...** *and* **Browse Help** *are the same as the buttons.*
▶ **Text Size** *lets you adjust the size of the text.*
▶ **Find (on this page)...** *opens a dialog box where you can type in a word to search for on the current page only. This can be useful as some pages are rather long.*

▶ **Settings...** *controls the access to the online Help. This is also present on the Online/Offline Help button – which we met earlier.*

5.7 Application Help

The utilities and applications that are supplied as part of Windows 7 have Help systems which follow the same pattern as the main Help and Support system. It's the same window and the links, Search facility and other routines are exactly the same, though the initial page and the way into the system do vary.

1 *If there is a menu bar, look for* **Help** *on the far right. You will normally use the first item on this menu, which will be called* **Help Topics** *or* **Contents** *or something similar.*

2 *If there is no menu bar, look for a* 🔘 *icon and click that.*

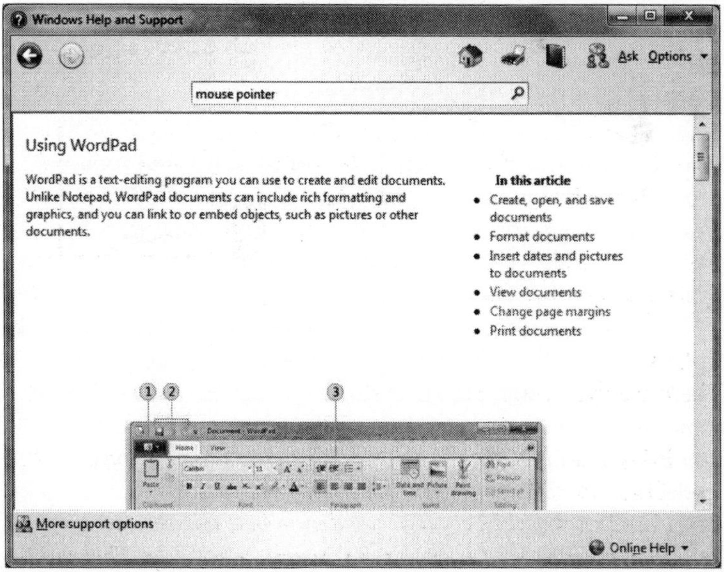

Figure 5.11 The initial Help page for WordPad.

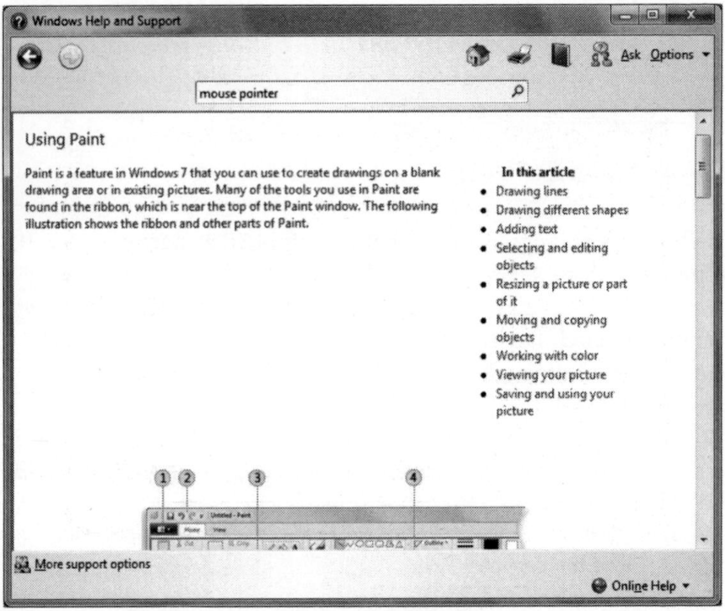

Figure 5.12 The initial Help page for Paint.

NON-WINDOWS HELP SYSTEMS

Other applications from Microsoft or other software producers also have their own Help systems. These vary in style and presentation, but normally behave in much the same way.

Contents

A Help system can be thought of as a book, with a different topic on every page – though, unlike paper books, the pages vary in length. Related topics are arranged into chapters, and the whole book is extensively indexed. But this is a reference book. Don't attempt to read it all from start to finish, you'll just give yourself a headache.

Help systems normally open at the **Contents** tab – if another tab is at the front, click on the **Contents** label to switch to it. Use this tab to get an overview of the available Help, and when you want to read around a topic. Initially, only the main section names will be visible.

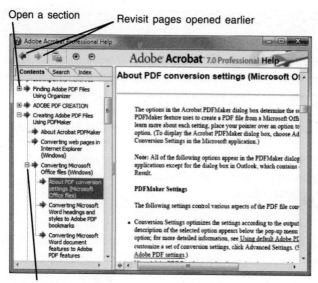

Open a section   Revisit pages opened earlier

Close the section

Figure 5.13 The Help system of a non-Windows 7 application.

▶ *Beside each section name is a ⊞ icon. Click on the section name or the icon to open the section.*

▶ *Some sections have subsections. Again, click on the name or ⊞ to open one.*

▶ *When you see a list of topic pages, click on the name to display a page in the right-hand panel of the window.*

▶ *You can usually only open one section at a time – the open one will close when you select another. If you want to close a section, click the ⊟ icon.*

▶ *As you browse through the system, the* **Back** *and* **Forward** *buttons become active, allowing you to return to pages that you have opened earlier in that session.*

You can navigate around an application Help system, as you can in Windows Help and Support, following links, and moving backwards and forwards.

Index

You will find a Search facility in non-Windows 7 Help systems, and it will work in just the same way as in Windows Help and Support. You will also find a third way of tracking down Help, that is not present in Windows. A Help **Index** works like the index in a book, with keywords listed in alphabetical order.

1 *Start to type a keyword into the box at the top. The list will scroll to bring into view words that start with those letters.*
2 *If the word you want is not yet visible, type more letters.*
3 *If an entry has* ⊞ *to the side, it has sub-entries. Click the icon to display them.*
4 *Select an entry to display the relevant page.*

▶ *In some systems, if an entry leads to several Help pages, you will see a* '**Topics Found**' *list – select one from here.*

Type the first letter(s) of the word

Click to display sub-entries

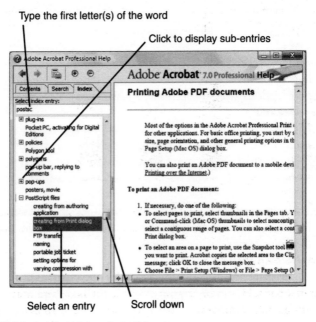

Select an entry   Scroll down

Figure 5.14 Using the Index tab in an application Help system.

Creating the Index

The first time that you use the Index, you may have to wait while the system scans the Help pages to create it.

5.8 Tips and prompts

TOOLTIPS

The icons on tool buttons are good *reminders* of the nature of the tool, but they are not always immediately obvious to the new user. Tooltips are little pop-up labels that tell you what icons stand for.

Wait a moment for a Tooltip

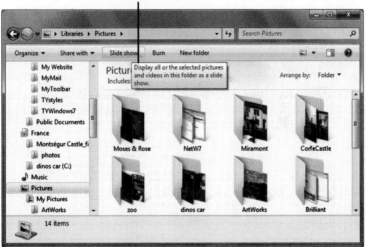

Figure 5.15 If you don't know what an icon does, point to it and wait a second. A Tooltip will appear, giving its name. If you still need Help with it, at least you now know what to look up in the Index.

STATUS BAR PROMPTS

The Status bar serves many purposes – it is through here that applications will communicate with you, so do keep an eye on it. In some applications it is used to display a brief description of items as you point to them in the menus.

THINGS TO REMEMBER

▶ *You can get into Windows' Help and Support system from the option on the Start menu.*

▶ *To browse through Help and Support, pick a topic from the headings on the Home page.*

▶ *To find Help and Support on a specific topic run a Search.*

▶ *Troubleshooters can be helpful in solving problems.*

▶ *Additional Help is available online.*

▶ *The Help systems in applications may look different from Windows Help and Support but are used in much the same way. Browse through the Contents or track down specific Help pages through the Index or Search tabs.*

▶ *Tooltips and Status bar prompts can help you to get to grips with the tools and commands in a new application.*

SELF TEST

1 *Where do you start to get Help with Windows?*

2 *If you are completely new to Windows, where is the best place to start in the Help System?*

3 *On a Help page what is the meaning of:*
   A *A blue rectangle beside a heading?*
   B *Green text?*
   C *A small black arrow beside a heading?*

4 *What might you find in a non-Windows Help system, that you will not find in any in the Windows set?*

5 *What's a Tooltip? How do you get to see one?*

6

The Desktop

6.1 Personalize your Desktop

You can change the colour scheme, the background, the mouse pointers, the sounds and other aspects of your PC. You may not want to tackle all of them at one sitting, but that's not a problem. You can change any of the settings whenever and as often as you like. If the PC has several users, then they can all have their own Desktop settings which will be applied when they log on. Feel free to experiment – it's your Desktop.

1 *Right-click anywhere on the background of the Desktop.*
2 *Select* **Personalize** *from the menu.*
3 *The* **Personalize** *window will open. The main panel holds links to the main routines for customizing the Desktop. Note also the links at the top and bottom of the sidebar on the left.*

The instructions in the next few sections all assume that you have reached this point.

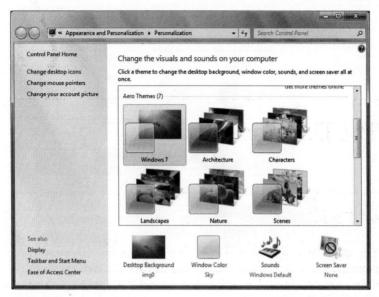

Figure 6.1 The Personalize window.

6.2 Themes

By selecting a new theme, you can change the colours, background images and sounds in one fell swoop, and they will (in theory) work together to create a harmonious atmosphere...

To change the theme:
1 *Scroll through the display to see what's there.*
2 *Click on one if you think it might work. The theme will be applied in a few seconds.*
3 *If you don't like the effect, try another. You can change the theme whenever and as often as you like.*

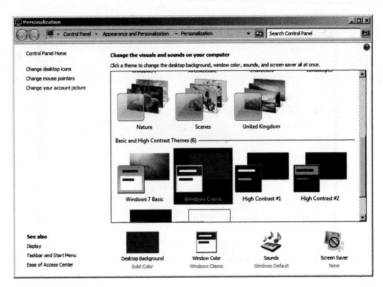

Figure 6.2 Choosing a theme. If you can't see anything you like here, you can get more themes online, and you can change any aspect of the theme later.

6.3 Window Color

Use this panel to set the style, colour and fonts for the Desktop and standard Windows elements in all applications – the window frames, menus, dialog boxes, etc.

The initial display is concerned with colour and transparency. There are seven preset colours, but you can also mix your own.

1 *Select* **Window Color.**
2 *Pick a colour, or click* **Show color mixer** *and adjust the* **Hue, Saturation** *and* **Brightness** *levels to get the desired mix.*
3 *If you want transparent window frames, tick* **Enable transparency** *and drag the slider to set the level.*

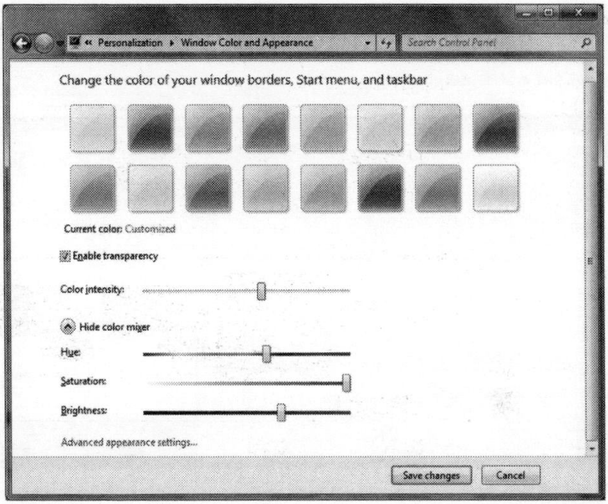

Figure 6.3 Setting the colour. The advanced appearance settings only apply to the Basic and high contrast schemes.

Basic and high contrast schemes

4 *If you have selected Windows Basic, or a high contrast scheme, the Window Color option opens a dialog box where you can set the colour, font and size of individual elements.*

5 *Click on an item in the preview pane, or select it from the* **Item** *list, then set its size, colour and font as required.*

6 *Click* **OK** *to return to the* **Properties** *panel.*

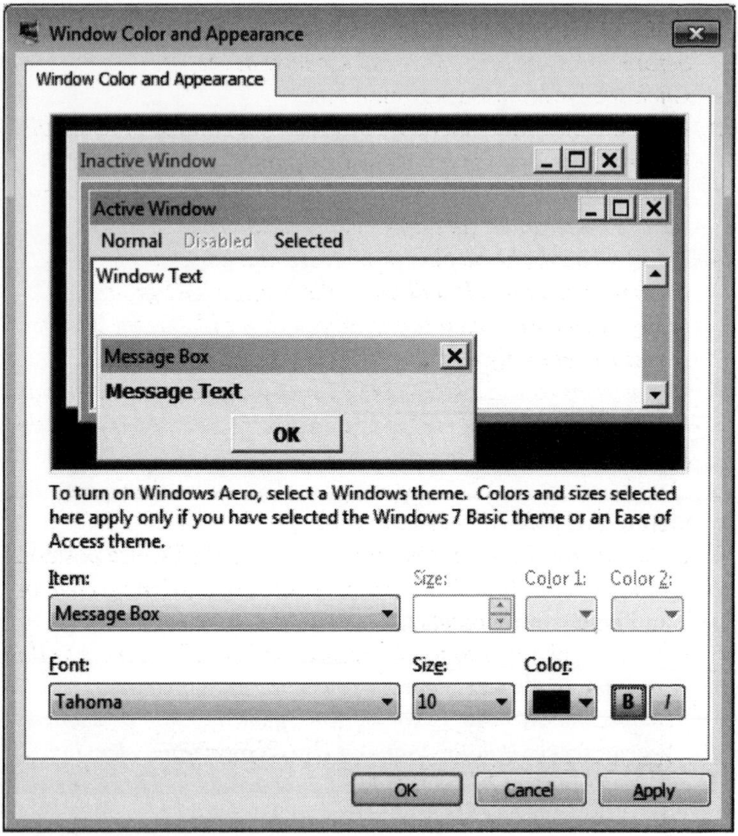

Figure 6.4 The Window Color and Appearance dialog box.

6.4 The Background

The background is purely decorative! The background can be a plain colour, a full screen picture or a small image 'tiled' to fill the whole screen. You can even have a set of pictures running in a slide show. Windows 7 has a selection of small and large images, but more or less any image can be used.

1. *Make sure that as much background as possible is visible before you start this – you will see why at Step 4.*
2. *Click the **Desktop Background** link.*
3. *Click the button by **Picture Locations** to get a list of available folders. (The **Browse** button will let you reach any folder in your system, but you might want to leave this until after you have learned about files and folders in the next chapter.)*
4. *Scroll through the display of pictures and click on one if it catches your fancy. It will be applied to the background so that you can see how it looks. If you don't like it, try another. A picture will only be fixed in place if you click **OK**.*
5. *If you want to use a set of images as a slide show, hold down the [Ctrl] button and click on each one in turn (or click on the folder name to select all of the images in it.)*
6. *If you have selected several images, drop down the **Change picture every:** list and set the time.*
7. *If the picture is smaller than the screen, use the **Picture position** option at the bottom left to either **Stretch** it to fill the screen, or **Tile** it across and down, or **Center** it in its natural size.*
8. *Click Save changes to fix the choice, or **Cancel** to revert to the current background.*

Figure 6.5 Setting a new background.

Use your photos

Come back to this after you have stored some of your own digital photos on the computer, and set your own favourite picture(s) as the background.

6.5 The screen saver

This is mainly decorative. A screen saver is a moving image that takes over the screen if the computer is left unattended for a while. On older monitors this prevented a static image from burning a permanent ghost image into the screen. Newer monitors do not suffer from this, and in fact, most now have an energy saving feature that turns them off when they are not in use. If your monitor has this, the screen saver will only be visible briefly, if at all.

A screen saver can be password protected (or revert to the log-on screen if there are several users), so that it will lock your PC until the password is entered. This can be useful if you do not want passers-by to read your screen while you are away from your desk – it is like putting Lock on automatic, with a time delay.

1 *In the* **Personalize** *window, select* **Screen Saver.**
2 *Pick a saver from the drop-down list – check the preview to see how it will look.*
3 *With some savers you can set the speed, colour, text or other features. Click the* **Settings** *button to see if there are options.*
4 *Set the* **Wait** *time – how long does the computer have to be idle before the screen saver should kick in?*
5 *If you want to protect your PC, tick the* **On resume, display logon screen** *checkbox.*

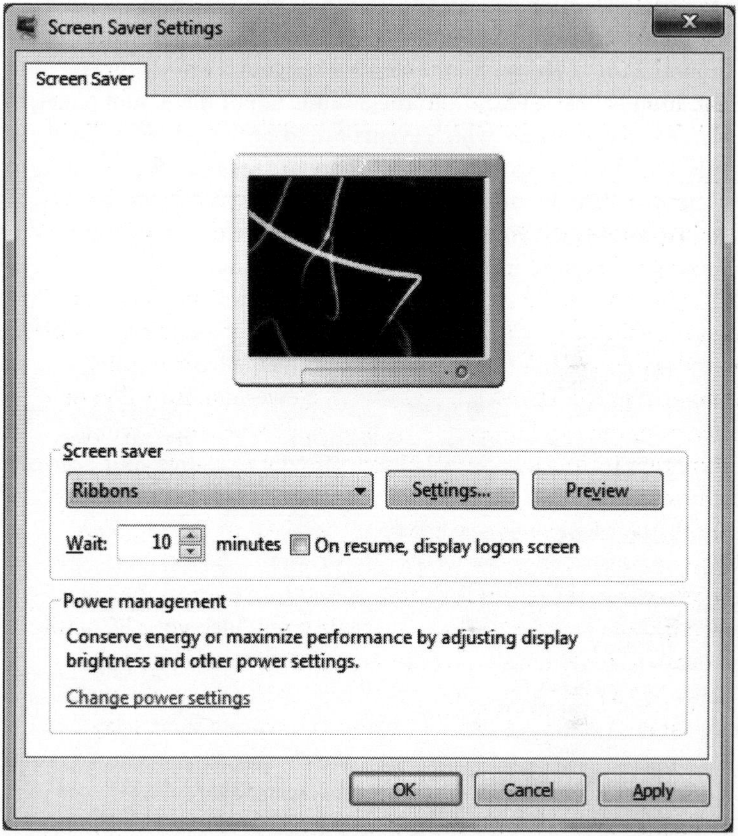

Figure 6.6 The screen saver dialog box. Click the Change power settings link to set the times that the system should wait before shutting down the monitor and the hard drive. Don't make these waits too short. Turning a monitor on and off constantly may reduce its lifespan.

6.6 Sounds

Windows attaches sounds to certain events so that you get, for example, a fanfare at start up and a warning noise when you are about to do something you may later regret. Some of these are just for fun, others can be very useful. If you tend to watch the keyboard, rather than the screen, when you are typing, then an audible warning can help to alert you to a situation before it becomes a problem.

The **Sounds** link leads you to the **Sounds** tab of the **Sound** panel, where you can decide which events are to be accompanied by a sound, and which sounds to use. There are several schemes and a selection of individual sounds supplied with Windows, or you can use your own .wav files. (You can create these with Sound Recorder – explore it one day, it's simple to use.)

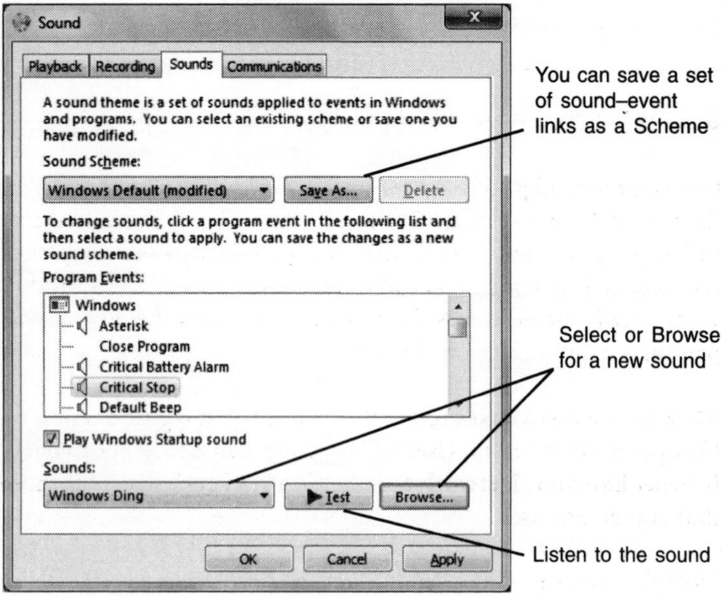

Figure 6.7 Selecting a new sound to attach to an event. If you want to turn off a sound, select 'None' in the sounds list.

1   *In the* **Personalize** *window, select* **Sounds.**
2   *If you want to change the overall style of your sounds, select a scheme from the list.*
3   *To change the sound assigned to an event, select the program event from the list then either pick a sound from the* **Sounds** *list, or click* **Browse** *and locate the file on your hard disk.*
4   *Click* [▶ **Test**] *to hear the current sound.*
5   *When you have finished, click* **OK.**
Or
6   *Click* **Save As...** *if you want to save the scheme so that it can be reapplied later.*

6.7 Desktop icons

Over on the top left of the Personalize window are three Tasks and the first of these is **Change Desktop Icons.** The icons are shortcuts to key programs and folders. Initially you may find that only the Recycle Bin (which you can use to recover deleted files) and Computer (which displays the disks and drives on the PC) may be present – it depends upon the installation.

Click on the checkboxes to toggle the display of the icons for Computer, Recycle Bin, User's Files (your own document folder), Internet Explorer, Network and the Control Panel. Turn off those that you do not use.

Note that you can select new images for some icons – select the icon, then click **Change Icon** and pick a different image.

There may not be many icons on your Desktop yet, but when you install applications, these will often add their own icons. And you can create your own shortcuts – we will come back to this in the next chapter.

Figure 6.8 Selecting the desktop icons to display.

6.8 Mouse pointers

These options are purely decorative, though anything which makes it easier to see what you are doing must be beneficial. There are a dozen or so pointers, each related to a different mouse action. You can pick a whole new scheme or change individual pointers.

1 *In task list on the left of the Personalize window, select* **Mouse Pointers**.
2 *Drop down the* **Scheme** *list and select a scheme. The icons in the display will change to match.*
3 *To change an individual pointer, select it and click* **Browse**. *You can then pick a new one from the Cursors folder.*

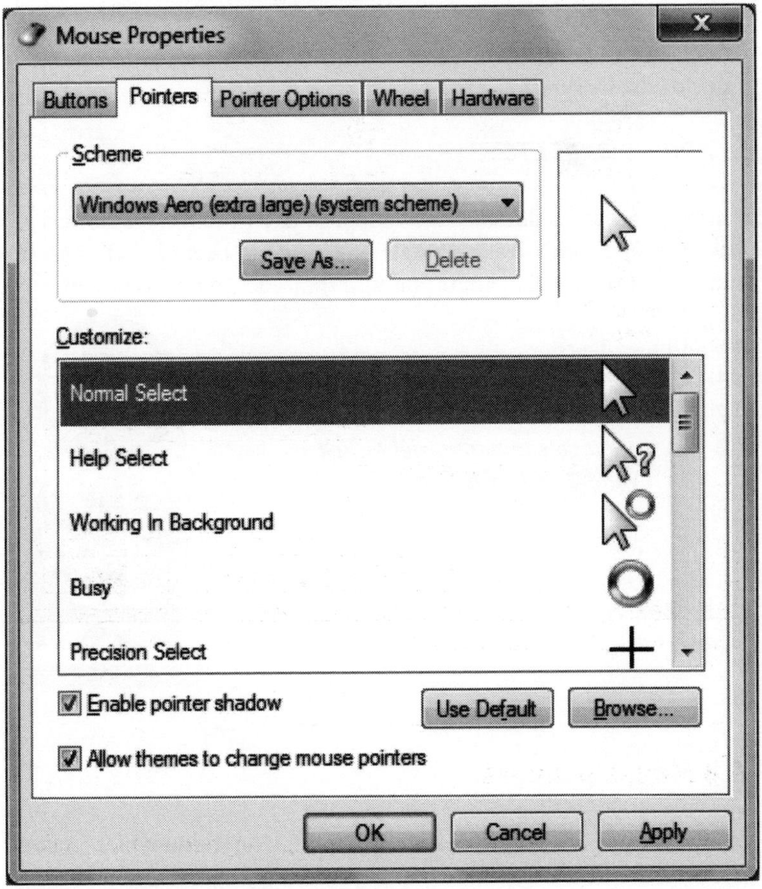

Figure 6.9 Changing the mouse pointers. If you have a customized set that you might want to reapply in future, click Save As... and save it. It will then be added to the scheme list.

6.9 Gadgets

Gadgets are mini-applications that you can add to your Desktop.
Some are handy utilities, some the latest news headlines, stock
reports or weather forecasts from the Web, others are just for fun.
All are worth exploring.

The gadgets are normally shown in the Sidebar, which sits on the
right of the Desktop.

ADDING GADGETS

There are around a dozen gadgets supplied as part of the Windows 7
package, and more available online. These can be added at any
time – and removed again if you find that you do not use them.

To add a gadget:
1 *Right-click anywhere on the screen.*
2 *Select* **Gadgets.**
3 *At the gadgets window, right-click
  on a gadget and select* **Add.**

Figure 6.10 Adding a gadget.

Gadgets can be customized and/or controlled, but in different ways, depending upon what they are.

They all have a mini-toolbar which appears when you point to the top right. It has three parts: a Close button, an Options button and a Handle which is used for moving it.

— Close
— Options
— Handle

THE CLOCK

With the clock, you can change the face, name and the time zone. (You can have several clocks, each set to a different time zone, in which case the name could identify the location.)

1 *Point to the top right to get the toolbar and click the* **Options**
  button – the **Clock options** *dialog box will appear.*
2 *Use the arrows to cycle through the choice of faces until you*
  find the one you prefer.
3 *If you have several clocks, type in a* **name** *to suit the location.*
4 *Select a* **time zone.**
5 *Tick* the **Show the second hand** *box, if it is wanted.*
6 *Click* OK.

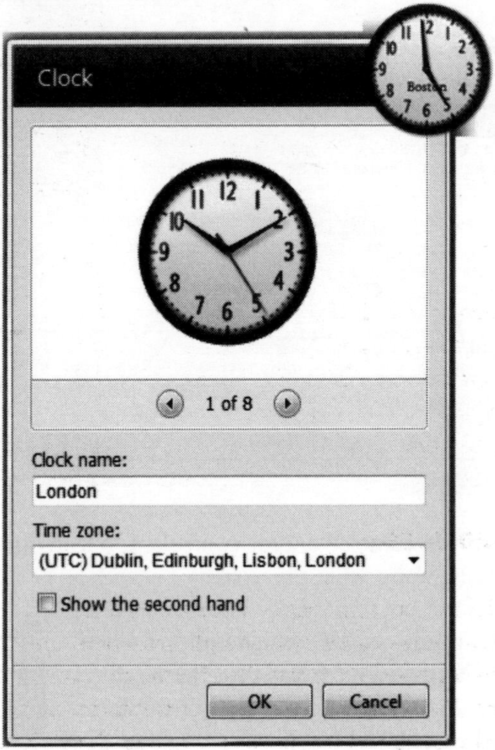

Figure 6.11 Setting the options for the Clock.

THE CALENDAR

This can show the day's date or the whole month. Its only option is size: larger shows the month and the day, smaller just shows the day.

In month mode:

1 *Click on the arrows at the top left and right to switch to previous and later months.*
2 *Click on any day to display that day only.*

In day mode:

1 *If the current date is not showing, the bottom left corner will be turned up. Click on this to display today's date.*
2 *Click anywhere else on the calendar to switch to month mode.*

FEED HEADLINES

Feeds are brief notices sent out by websites to alert you to new material as it appears on the site. Initially, you will only have a choice of four feeds from Microsoft, offering differing mixtures of news and tips. You can add new feeds through Internet Explorer. You can set the gadget to display any single feed, or all of them.

To set up the feeds:

1 *Point to a spot to the top right of the gadget to display the mini toolbar, and click the* **Options** *button.*
2 *Select the feed to displays, and the number to show at a time.*
3 *Click* **OK**.

To read feeds:

1 *Use the up and down arrows at the bottom to scroll through the headlines.*

2 *Click on a headline to display a summary of the story.*

3 *Click on the summary title if you want to read the full story online. It will pass the link to the browser and download the story from the Web.*

Figure 6.12 Reading feed stories.

SLIDE SHOW

This is purely decorative. It will cycle through the images in any chosen folder, showing each one for a set length of time.

View

If you want a closer look at a picture, there's a View tool that will open it in the Photo Gallery (see page 266) – point to anywhere on the gadget to make the toolbar appear.

The folder, display time and transition between pictures are set in the options dialog box.

PICTURE PUZZLE

This is a sliding block puzzle, and can consume hours of your time if you are not careful – it's not as easy as you might think!

Click on any block adjacent to the space to move that block into it.

The options dialog box offers a dozen images to pick from.

6.10 Gadget controls

These apply to all gadgets. Right-click on a gadget to display its menu of controls.

There are only half a dozen. **Add Gadgets, Options** and **Close Gadget** are obvious. The rest are worth a closer look.

▶ **Detach from Sidebar** – *when a gadget is detached, it initially goes to the top left of the Desktop, though it can be dragged from there to anywhere on screen. Some gadgets become larger when detached – Calendar shows the month and the day, Slide Show, Feed Headlines and other information displays become twice the size.*

▶ **Move** – *selects the gadget so that you can move it within the Sidebar. To move it, you need to drag on the handle. Note: you can drag on the handle without using Move, and you can drag it off the Sidebar, detaching it, if you like.*

▶ **Opacity** – *the gadgets can be distracting. If you reduce their opacity and make them more transparent, they are less eye catching. When you point to one, it becomes solid once more.*

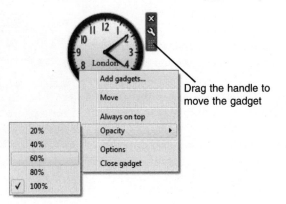

Drag the handle to move the gadget

Figure 6.13 Setting the opacity level.

THINGS TO REMEMBER

▶ *You can personalize your Desktop to suit yourself.*

▶ *The Color and Appearance options set the colour and transparency of the display.*

▶ *The Background and Screen Saver options are largely decorative and have little impact on the working of your system.*

▶ *There are several sets of mouse pointers that you can choose from.*

▶ *You can change the sounds attached to events.*

▶ *The Display Settings are normally best left at their defaults.*

▶ *There are half a dozen standard icons which you can display on your Desktop if you use them.*

▶ *You can fill your Desktop with gadgets – and some of them may even be useful!*

SELF TEST

1 *What's the simplest way to get to the Personalization window?*

2 *The theme controls which aspects of the Desktop?*

3 *If you do not like transparent window frames, can you do anything to change them?*

4 *How can you get the background picture to change automatically?*

5 *What is the point of a screen saver?*

6 *How can you add more gadgets to the Desktop?*

7 *And how can you remove any you do not use?*

7

Files and folders

7.1 Disks and folders

To be able to use your computer efficiently, you must know how to manage your files – how to find, copy, move, rename and delete them – and how to organize the folders on your disks. In Windows, these jobs are done through Windows Explorer. In this chapter we will have a look at this vital program and see how it is used for file and folder management. We will also look at creating links between documents and applications, and at the Recycle Bin – a neat device which makes it much less likely that you will delete files by accident.

A typical hard drive can hold 200 Gigabytes of data – enough for around 50 movies, or over 250,000 high-resolution digital photographs, or a couple of thousand full length novels, or huge quantities of whatever it is you want to store. Obviously, with this much storage space, it must be organized if you are ever to find anything. The organization comes through *folders* and *libraries*.

A folder is an elastic-sided division of the disk. It can contain any number of files and subfolders – which can contain other subfolders, and so on ad infinitum. The structure is sometimes described as a tree. The *root* is at the drive level. The main folders branch off from here, and each may have a complex set of branches leading from it. At the simplest, a C: drive might contain three folders – *Program Files* (with subfolders for each application), *Users* (with subfolders for each user) and *Windows* (which has subfolders for the sets of programs and files that make up the Windows 7 system). You can create new folders, and rename, delete or move them to produce your own structure.

A library looks and behaves very like a folder, but is actually a set of links to one or more folders, which may be scattered through your system. The purpose of libraries is to bring stuff together for ease of access. The Pictures library on my machine, for instance, has My Pictures folder, the Public Pictures folder and another folder of photos that is stored elsewhere on the C: drive. I can also add my camera's own storage, other folders on the PC or on any other PC on the local network. If I want to do anything with all of my pictures, such as backing them up, I only need to go to the Pictures library.

7.2 Windows Explorer

Unlike every other Windows application, Windows Explorer (or Explorer for short) does not have its name in the title bar, and it is rarely started by name. We noted earlier that documents are associated with applications, which will start when you open the document. In exactly the same way, Explorer is associated with folders and the normal way of starting it is to open a folder.

▶ *Open the* **Start** *menu and click* **Computer**. *This will run Explorer and open the* **Computer** *folder, which holds all the disk drives on your system.*

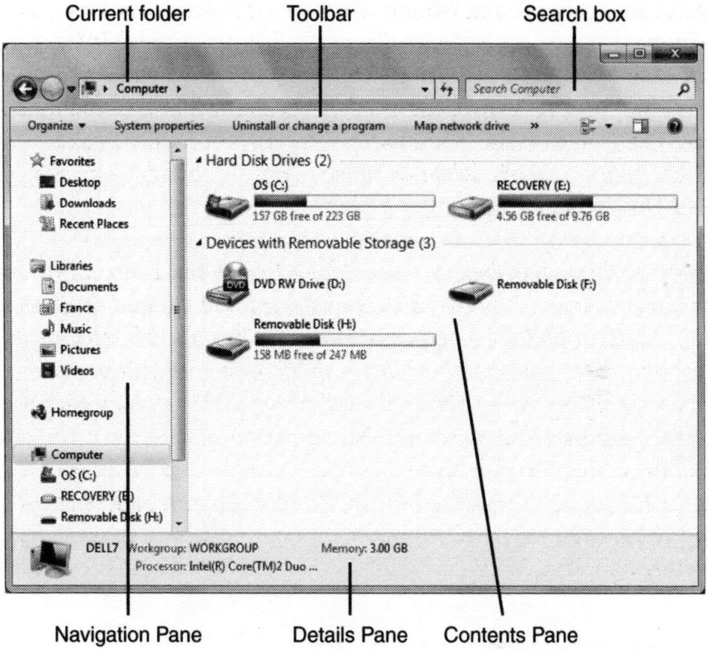

Figure 7.1 Explorer showing computer. This is the default display.

The Explorer display is highly variable. Some elements can be turned on or off, and some change in response to the material that is currently displayed. These are always present:

▶ The **Current Folder** box shows you where you are now.
▶ The **Search** box can be used to hunt for a file (see page 145).
▶ The **Toolbar** buttons vary according to what sort of folder is displayed, and what sort of file, if any, is selected at the time.
▶ The **Contents Pane** usually shows the files and folders in the current folder, though for Computer it shows the disks and other storage on the PC.

These are optional, though the first two are normally present.

- ▶ *The* **Navigation Pane** *lists the disks, libraries, and folders on your system. Use this to move between the libraries and folders.*
- ▶ *The* **Details Pane** *tells you the size, date and other details about the selected file or folder.*
- ▶ *The* **Preview Pane** *shows a small version of an image or the first page of other documents, if a preview is available.*
- ▶ *The* **Menu bar** *gives another way to reach the commands and options. Compared to the selected and context-sensitive Toolbar, which changes as you work, this has the advantage that every command is always there, and in the same place.*

To turn the optional panes and **Menu bar** on or off:

1 *Click on the* **Organize** *button. Point to* **Layout** *and click on an element to toggle its display.*

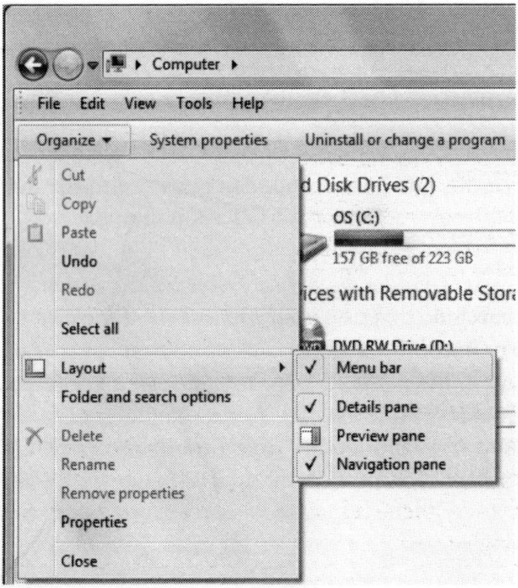

Figure 7.2 The Layout options. If an element is turned on, it will have a tick.

2 *If you turn on the Preview Pane in* Computer, *there will be nothing to see. Let's find something. Click* Documents *in the Libraries list.*
3 *Check that the Preview Pane is present – it may not be, as Explorer opens each folder with the same display as was used previously. Turn it on if necessary.*
4 *Select a file and see if it has a preview.*
5 *The preview will be scaled to fit the Preview Pane. If you want to change the size of the pane, drag on the divider.*

Back – return to the last folder you viewed   Menu bar

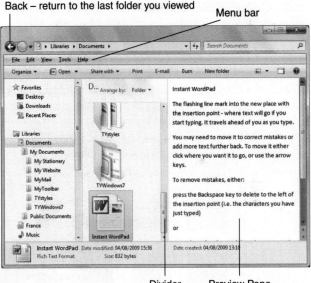

Divider   Preview Pane

Figure 7.3 If the window is too small the Preview Pane cannot be opened.

It's your Explorer

The layout of Explorer can be changed at any point. Experiment with it until you find the layout that works best for you – then stick with it, so that you know where everything is!

7.3 View options

Files and folders can be shown as Icons, ranging in size from **Small** to **Extra Large, List, Details or Tiles.** The display is controlled through the **Views** button on the toolbar.

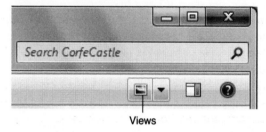

Views

Figure 7.4 Click the button to cycle through the alternative views, or click the arrow to open the menu.

Figure 7.5 Click an option or drag the slider to change the view and icon size.

The **icons** views show – if possible – an image of each file, and otherwise an icon to identify its type. They work best, of course, with images, but documents with previews can also be displayed. Make the icons as large as you need to be able to identify files.

Small Icons and **List** differ mainly in the order of the icons – **Icons** lists across the screen and leaves more space between them. Both are good for selecting sets of files.

Details gives a column display of *properties* under the headings Name, Type, Size, Tags, Date modified and others (these vary – see *Choose Details* below). Every file has properties. Some of these are set by the system, e.g. its type, size, date modified, and others can be changed by you, e.g. its name and where it is stored. Some properties are common to all types of files, but some types have additional properties that hold further information.

Tiles displays for each file a large icon (so it is easy to identify the type), plus details of its type and size.

To change the view:

1 *Click the* **Views** *button to cycle between the main types.*
Or
  2 *Click the arrow beside the Views button to see the options.*
  3 *Click on a name to select a view.*
Or
  4 *Drag the slider to adjust the size – you can stop part-way between two set views to get an intermediate size.*

VIEW MENU OPTIONS

If you turn on the Menu Bar,
you will have some additional
layout and view options. Two
are well worth knowing about:
Status Bar, near the top of the
menu, and Choose Details, near
the bottom.

Status Bar

If it has been turned on, the
Status Bar lies at the bottom
of the window and shows the
number of objects in the folder
and the amount of memory they
use, or the size of a selected file.

▶ *Open the* View *menu and
tick* Status Bar *to turn it on.*

File	Edit	View	Tools	Help

Organize ▾

- Toolbars ▶
- Status bar
- Explorer Bar ▶
- Extra large icons
- ● Large icons
- Medium icons
- Small icons
- List
- Details
- Tiles
- Content
- Hide file names
- Arrange by ▶
- Sort by ▶
- Group by ▶
- Choose details...
- Go To ▶
- Refresh

Choose Details

In Details view, you can choose which properties to include in the
headings. As well as showing you different information about files,
this also affects the way that you can sort and group files in any
view – see section 7.7, *Sorting and filtering files*.

1 *Right-click anywhere along the headings. The menu lists the
more important properties.*
2 *Click on a property name to toggle the tick on or off.*
3 *If you can't see the property you want to include, click*
More...

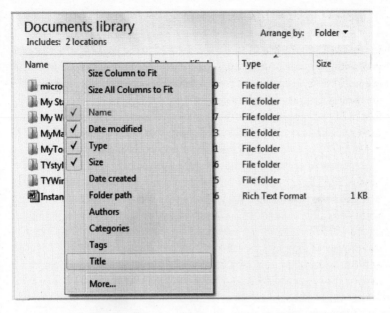

4 At the **Choose Details** *dialog box, tick the details you want to include.*

5 *The order of the columns in the display matches the order in this list. Select a detail and use the* **Move Up** *and* **Move Down** *buttons to rearrange its order if required.*

6 *Click* **OK**.

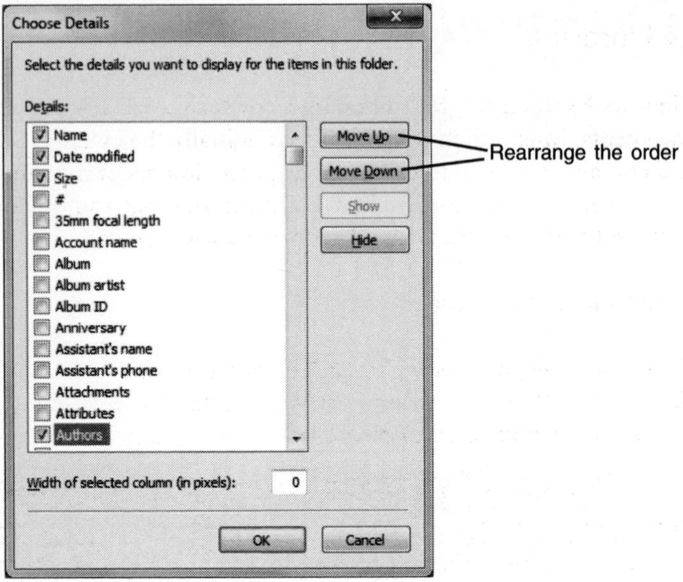

Figure 7.6 Different types of files have different details which can be displayed. Rearrange the order.

Menus when you need them

If the Menu bar is turned off, you can make it pop open if you want to use one of the commands. Press [Alt] and the bar will appear and stay open while you select the command, or until you press [Alt] again.

7.4 Libraries

Windows Explorer has four libraries ready for your use – Documents, Music, Pictures and Videos. Initially they will each contain your own folders and the public folders of the same names. You can add more folders or remove any that you do not want, and you can create new libraries if they are needed.

To add a folder to a library:

1 *In the Navigation pane, select the library.*
2 *On the left of the headers is the label* **Includes** *and a link marked* **X locations**. *Click the link.*

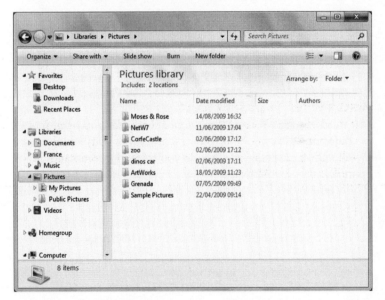

Figure 7.7 When you add a (location) folder to a library, you also add any folders within it. These are displayed by the library, which is why this one has eight folders in its list, but only two locations.

3 *A dialog box will open, listing the locations in the library. Click the **Add** button.*

4 *Work through your system to find the folder you want to add. Select it.*

5 *Click* **Include folder.**

6 *Back at the dialog box, click* **OK.**

ARRANGING FILES IN A LIBRARY

The files in a library are normally listed by folder, but can be arranged in different ways. The choice of ways depends upon the types of files stored in it, for example, in the Documents library, files can be arranged by author, date, tag, type and name.

1 *In the header line, click the button to the right of the* **Arrange by** *label.*
2 *Click on the item that you want to arrange the files by.*

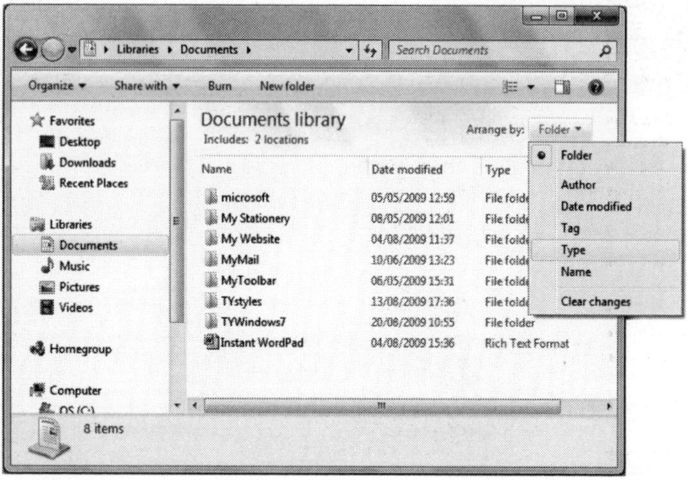

Figure 7.8 Different arrangements allow you to sort and group files in different ways. See also section 7.7.

CREATING A NEW LIBRARY

When you are working on a project – especially one that uses a mixture of documents, pictures and other types of files, created by several applications – you may find it useful to set up a library to bring all the project's folders together.

1 *Select* Libraries *in the Navigation pane.*
2 *Click the* New library *button on the Toolbar.*
3 *Give the new library a name to identify it.*

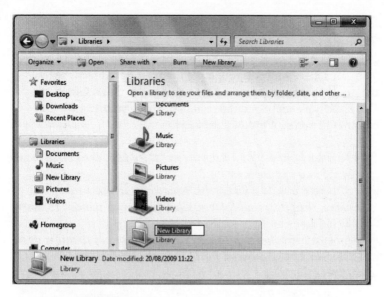

4 Click on the folder to open it.
5 It will initially be empty. Click **Include a folder** to add your first location.

6 Add more folders, as needed, using the method that you saw earlier.

7.5 Folders

You can access folders through the libraries, and directly through the drives that they are stored on – and notice that a CD-ROM, DVD, memory stick, and the memory card in your camera all count as drives in Windows Explorer.

▶ *To open a library or a drive to see its folders, click on its name in the Navigation pane.*
▶ *If there is a little white arrowhead to the left of a folder's name, then it has subfolders. Click on the arrowhead to open the folder.*
▶ *A black arrowhead to the left of a folder shows that it is open. Click on the arrowhead to close up the subfolders.*

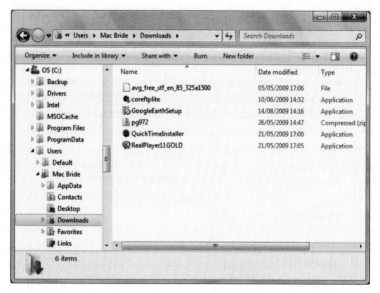

Figure 7.9 Here the Downloads folder, in my storage area, has been selected.

Folders in libraries and on drives

It can be a little confusing at first sight, having the same folder in two places, but just remember that libraries only hold links to folders. Most of the time, it don't really matter whether you are working directly in the folder, or reaching it through a library. Most of your work with files is done from within applications – this is where you save and open them – and applications can handle the details of file storage for you.

ORGANIZING FOLDERS

Windows sets up four folders for you to start with: *My Documents, My Music, My Pictures and My Videos*. These are unlikely to be enough for very long. You may need to create folders if:

▶ *You will be storing more than a few dozen documents – it's hard to find stuff in crowded folders;*
▶ *Your documents fall into distinct categories – personal, hobbies, different areas of work, etc.*

It doesn't matter if you put documents of different types in the same folder. It might look untidy when you view it in Explorer – though sorting by Type will help to clarify. In practice, you mainly access your documents through applications, and when you open a file there, the **Open File** dialog boxes will normally only list those of the right type.

CREATING FOLDERS

A new folder can be created at any time, and at any point in the folder structure. Here's how:

1. *In Windows Explorer, select the library or the folder which will contain the new one, or select the drive letter for a new top-level folder.*
2. *Click the* **New Folder** *button on the Toolbar.*

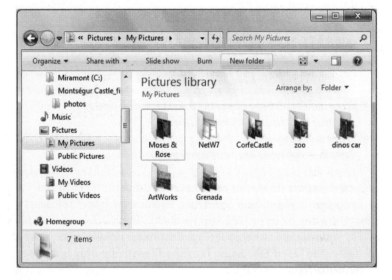

Or

3. *Open the* **File** *menu, point to* **New** *and select* **Folder.**
4. *Replace New Folder with a meaningful name.*

Folders are files

We think of folders as containers, but to the PC they are files, with lists of the names and disk locations of other files. They are special – you cannot read them – but they can be renamed, copied and deleted the same as document files.

SHORTCUTS TO FOLDERS

A Desktop shortcut offers a simple and quick way to open a folder – as long as you can see the Desktop! You can create new shortcuts in several ways. This is probably the easiest.

You need to be able to see the Desktop behind the Explorer window when you do this. If you have several windows open, click Show Desktop (at the far right of the Taskbar) to hide them, then bring the Explorer window back up. It needs to be in Restore mode.

1 *Select the folder in Explorer.*
2 *Hold down the right mouse button and drag the icon onto the Desktop. The label* **Move to Desktop** *will appear beside it. This is the default action, but if you are holding down the right mouse button, you have some options.*
3 *Release the button and a menu will appear. Select* **Create shortcuts here**.
4 *Click the icon to open the folder in Explorer.*

NAVIGATION BUTTONS

At the top left of the Explorer window are three buttons which you can use to go back to folders that you have already been in during the session. You can:

▶ *Go back to the last folder.*
▶ *Go forward again, after going back.*
▶ *Select a folder from the drop-down list.*

Back
Forward
Open list

7.6 Tags

Tags are a type of property that can be used to sort, filter and group files in Explorer displays. They give you a more flexible way of organizing files – I have found tags handy for classifying digital photos, but they can help in any situation where a file could fit into several categories.

Not all types of files can take tags. For example, you can add them to Word documents, other Microsoft Office files and JPEGs (the standard digital photo format) but not to text files, BMP images or Web pages.

1 *Make sure that the Details Pane is present in Explorer.*
2 *Select the document.*
3 *In the Details Pane, click where it says* **Tags:** Add a tag *– and if it doesn't say it, you can't add any.*

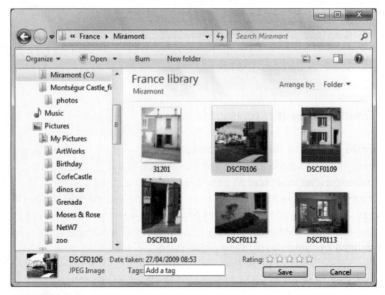

Figure 7.10 Starting to add a tag to a JPEG image.

4 *If this is the first time you have used the tag, type it in.*

5 *To add another tag, type a semicolon (;). Add a tag will reappear, and you are back to step 4.*

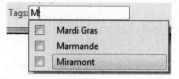

6 *Press* **Enter** *or click the* **Save** *button.*

7 *Tags are stored by the system. If you want to add a tag that you have already used for other files, type the first letter or two. Any that contain the same letters will be listed below the* **Tags** *box – click one to select. It will be written in for you and; "Add a tag" dropped in at the end, ready for the next.*

8 *Click back into the main display, or anywhere out of the Tags box to end.*

▶ *If you want to remove a tag at any point, select the file and click into the* **Tags** *box in the Details Pane.*

Editing tags

You cannot edit a tag once you have added it. If you decide it is not right, you must delete it and type a new one.

7.7 Sorting and filtering files

SORTING

You saw earlier that files in libraries could be arranged in different ways. There are more ways to sort and group files, though these only work when you are looking at the folders directly on the drive – not through a library – or if they have already been arranged by Name while viewing them in a library.

In folders, files are by default listed in name order, but they can be in order of any of their properties. This can be useful for tracking down files that you were working on at a certain date (but have forgotten the names), or for finding old or large files if you need to create some space.

If you are working in Details view, you can sort them by simply clicking on a heading. This will arrange them in ascending order by that property – click a second time to arrange them in descending order.

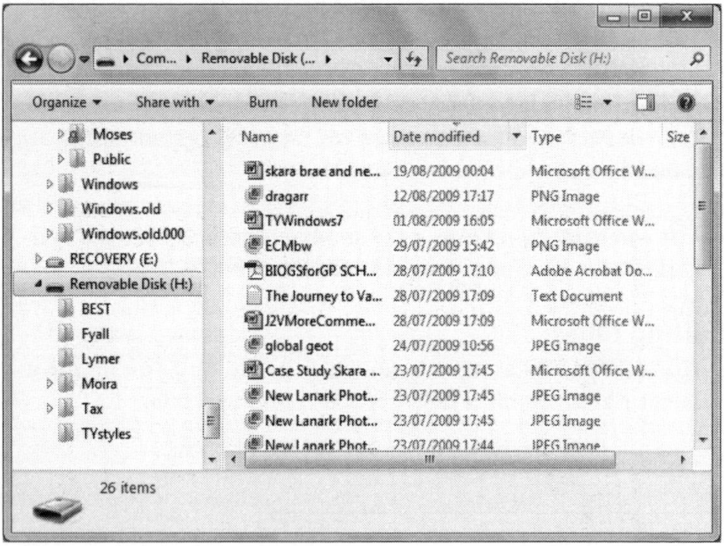

Figure 7.11 Click on a heading to sort files into order.

You can sort files in other views by using the Sort command on the View menu.

1 *If the Menu bar is not present, press* [**Alt**] *to open it.*
2 *Open the* **View** *menu, point to* **Sort by** *and select a property.*
3 *If you want to switch from* **Ascending** *to* **Descending** *order, open the* **View** *menu and point to* **Sort by** *again, and set the direction.*

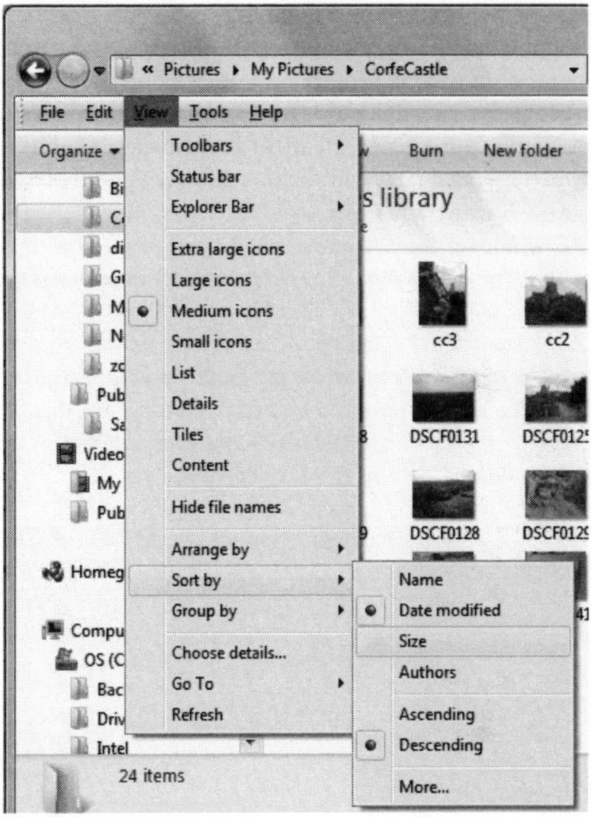

Figure 7.12 Using the View menu to sort files.

Sort before you select

When you are selecting a set of files, it is often a good idea to sort them first into the order that brings the ones you want close together.

FILTER

As the number of files in a folder or library increases, so it can get harder to find the one you want, And that where the filter comes in handy. If you point to a heading in Details view, you will notice a little down arrow to its right. Click on this and a menu will drop down, showing a list of tags or file types, alphabetical or size ranges, or whatever is appropriate to the property. You can use these to filter the display, so that only those from selected groups are shown.

1   *Click the down arrow on the property you want to use.*
2   *Tick those groups that you want to include – the display will change to show the selected ones and hide the rest.*
3   *Click anywhere off the menu to close it.*

Figure 7.13 Selecting groups of files to include.

Filter by name or size

Obviously names are unique, so you can't use them for grouping – instead files are grouped by alphabetical ranges. In the same way, size ranges are used for grouping.

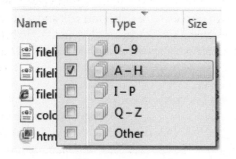

Filter by date

Filtering by date is different from filtering by other properties in that you can specify the date range. In all the rest, the filters are based on groups, and the ranges – if any – are set by Windows.

1 *Click the down arrow on the* **Date taken/modified** *heading.*
2 *To change the month, use the arrows either side of the month name to move backwards and forwards.*
3 *If you need to change the year, click on the* **Month–Year** *label and use the similar arrows there to move to another year. Click on the month name to display its days.*
4 *Click on a day to select it.*

Or

5 *Click on the first day, then hold down* [Shift] *and click on the last day to include.*
6 *Click anywhere on the main display to close the menu.*

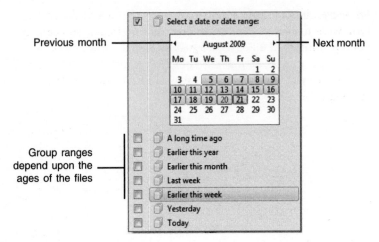

Previous month ———— August 2009 ———— Next month

Group ranges depend upon the ages of the files

Select a date or date range:

	August 2009	
Mo	Tu We Th Fr Sa Su	
	1 2	
3	4 5 6 7 8 9	
10	11 12 13 14 15 16	
17	18 19 20 21 22 23	
24	25 26 27 28 29 30	
31		

A long time ago
Earlier this year
Earlier this month
Last week
Earlier this week
Yesterday
Today

Figure 7.14 Setting a date range for filtering. The group ranges you are offered depend upon the ages of the files.

Clearing a filter

To restore the display so that all the files are included, you can either tick every box in the list or clear the ticks from them all – do whichever takes fewest clicks!

7.8 Folder types and options

Windows 7 has default settings for five different types of folders – those that hold mixed items, documents, pictures, music and videos. These settings affect the default display and toolbar buttons. They will have been applied to My Documents and the other ready-made folders. When you create a new folder within an existing one, e.g. one for this year's holiday snaps in My Pictures, the settings will be passed down to it. All this means that most of the time you don't need to bother about this.

However, if you create a new folder directly on a drive, or if you want to change the default display for a folder, you can set its type through the Properties panel.

To do this you must select the folder directly from the drive – not through a library.

1 *Right-click on a folder in the Folder list and select* **Properties.**

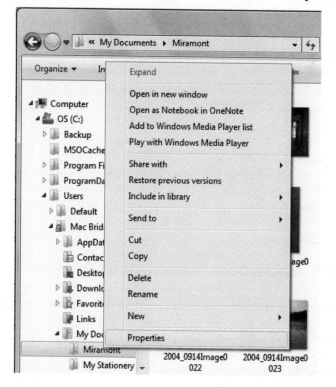

2 *At the* **Properties** *dialog box, switch to the* **Customize** *tab.*

3 *Drop down the folder type list and select the most suitable.*

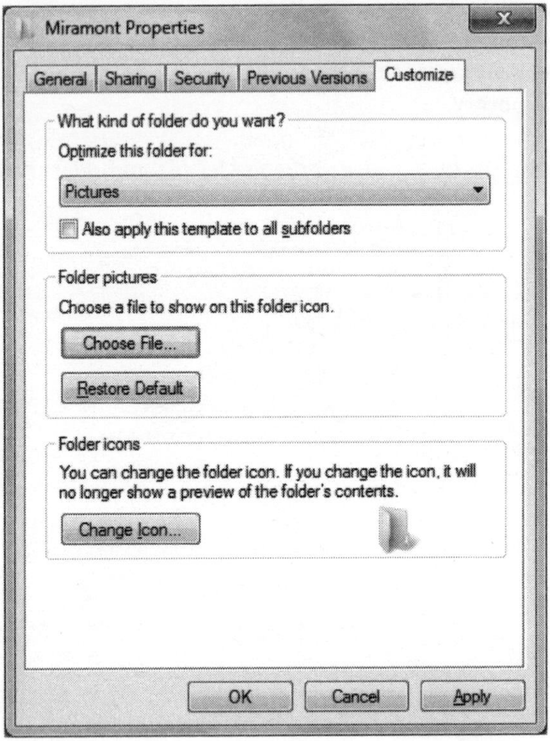

Figure 7.15 Check that a folder is set to the most appropriate type before looking at the folder options.
With some folder types you will see a Choose File... button which lets you choose an image to show on the
folder icon. There may be a Change Icon... option that will let you pick the icon for the folder.

FOLDER OPTIONS

The **Folder Options** affect how you view and manage your files and
folders. To reach the dialog box, open the **Tools** menu and select
Folder Options, or click the **Organize** button and select **Folder and
Search Options.**

General options
On the **General** tab, in the **Browse Folders** option, opening each
folder in its own window is useful for moving files from one to
another, but can produce a cluttered screen.

The **Click items as follows** settings apply to all files and folders, whether on the Desktop or in Windows Explorer.

The Navigation pane options make little real difference to the display – ignore them.

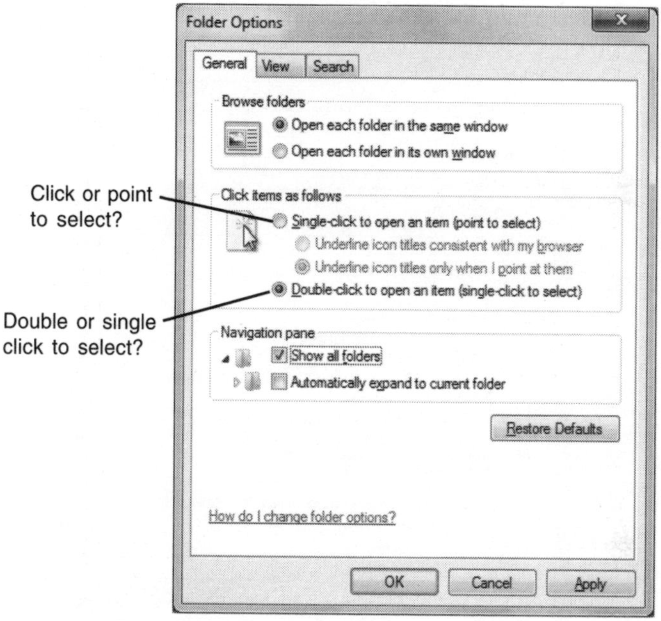

Click or point to select?

Double or single click to select?

Figure 7.16 The General tab of Folder Options.

View options
Some of the options here really are just fine-tuning, and you can come back and play with these when you want to see what they do. The more significant ones are covered here.

Most of the **Advanced Settings** should be left at their defaults until you have been using Windows for a while. A couple are worth checking now.

Hidden files – Windows 7 'hides' essential files, to prevent accidental deletion. They can be shown if needed, or these and system files – also crucial – can be hidden. For safety, hide them.

Hide empty drives in the Computer folder can save a little confusion if you have a number of removable drives.

Click **Apply to Folders** if you want the current settings – principally the choice of View – to be applied to all folders of this type. If you have got into a bit of a mess with your options (easily done!), click **Reset Folders** to go back to the original settings.

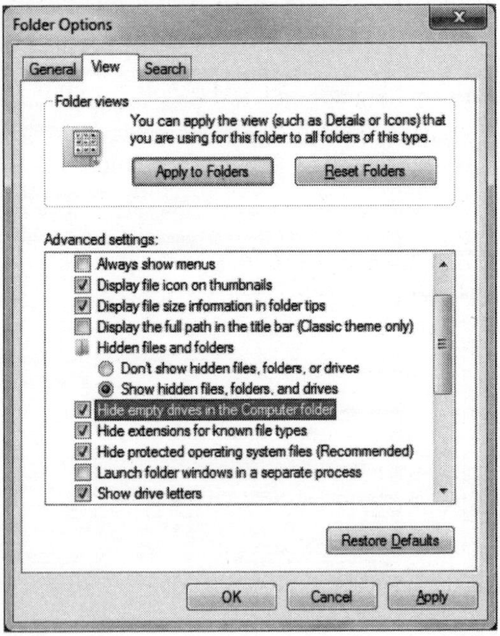

Figure 7.17 The View tab of Folder Options. Experiment with the options – if you don't like them click Restore Defaults to get back to normal.

Search options

Here you can specify what, how and when to search. Windows creates indexes for the documents that you create, and these store the author, tags, and other properties. The default search routine looks through these indexes, and through the names of other non-indexed files (mainly those of application and system programs).

In the **What to search** section, you can extend a search so that it also looks through the text of documents – very thorough, but rather slow, or restrict it to filenames – faster but you have to know some or all of the name.

In the **How to search** section the key option is probably **Find partial matches**. If this is on, the search can find files based on a few letters of a name or tag. The catch is, that it may find far too many that match those few letters.

Under **When searching non-indexed locations,** you would not normally want to search the system folders, but if you have stored documents in compressed folders, to save space, you may well want to search them.

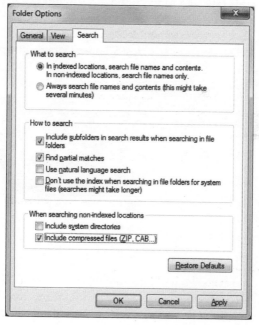

Figure 7.18 Setting the search options.

7.9 File associations

Documents are associated with applications, so that picking a document from a folder or from the Recent Items list on the Start menu will start up its application and open the document within it. But many types of documents can be opened by several different applications. The question is, which one to use? When applications are installed, the system records which types of files they can handle. It will normally make one program the default for each type of document. You can set a default program if there is not yet one in place, and you can change the existing defaults.

The simplest way to set or change default programs is to do it as needed, one file type at a time, from within Windows Explorer.

1 *Right-click on a document in the Contents Pane.*
2 *Point to* **Open With** *and select* **Choose Default Program...**

3 *The recommended programs – the ones Windows knows about – will be listed at the top. It may be possible to use others, but it's safest not to. Select the one to use.*

4 *Tick* **Always use the selected program** *to set it as the default.*
5 *Click* **OK.**

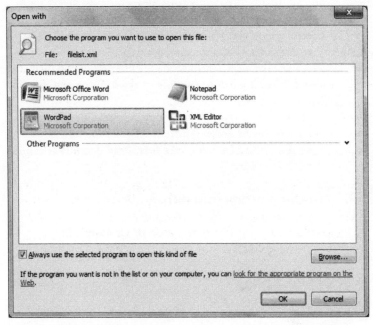

Figure 7.19 Choosing the default program for a file type.

7.10 File management

As a general rule, application files should be left well alone. Mess with these and your programs may not work. Document files are a different matter. They need to be managed actively or your folders will become cluttered, making it hard to find files.

SELECTING FILES

Before you can do anything with your files, you must select them.

▶ To select a single file, *point to it or click once on it (depending upon your Folder Options, see page 133).*
▶ To select a set of adjacent files, *if they are in a list or form a rectangular block, click to the side of the top one and drag an outline over the set.*

Or

▶ *Select the first, hold down* [**Shift**], *and select the last.*
▶ To select scattered files, *select the first, hold down* [**Ctrl**] *and select the rest in turn.*

Will arranging or sorting help?

Remember that files can be arranged in many different ways. If you sorted or grouped the files on a property would it make it easier to select them?

Figure 7.20 Adjacent files can be selected as a block.

Figure 7.21 Scattered files can also be selected together – it's fiddly, but still simpler than repeating operations on individual files.

MOVING AND COPYING FILES

Files can be easily moved or copied. The technique is similar for both.

1 *Select the file(s).*
2 *Scroll through the Folders display and/or open subfolders, if necessary, until you can see the target folder.*
3 *Drag the file(s) across the screen and over the target folder to highlight it, then drop the file(s) there.*
▶ *If the original and target folders are both on the same disk, this will move the selected file(s).*
▶ *If the folders are on different disks, or your target is a floppy disk, this will copy the file(s).*

To move a file from one disk to another, or copy within the same disk, hold down the right button while you drag. When you release the button, select **Move** or **Copy** from the context menu.

If you cannot see the target folder in the Folders list, open a second Explorer window and display it there, then drag the files across the screen between them.

Figure 7.22 If you can see the target folder, you can drag files into it.

Copy To Folder and Move To Folder

If your mouse control is a bit iffy, things can go astray when dragging files and folders. A slower, but more reliable alternative is to use the **Copy To Folder** and **Move To Folder** commands.

1 *Select the file(s).*
2 *To move a file, open the* **Edit** *menu (press* [**Alt**] *to open the Menu bar if needed) and select* **Move to Folder...**

Or

3 *To copy, open the* **Edit menu** *and select* **Copy to Folder…**

4 *The* **Move/Copy Items** *dialog box will open. Work your way down through the folder structure and select the target folder, then click* **OK**.

> **Move Items**
>
> Select the place where you want to move these 5 items, then click the Move button.
>
> ◢ 🖼 Pictures
> ◢ 🖼 My Pictures
>   📁 2008cahors
>   📁 2008garonne
>   📁 2009July
>   📁 ArtWorks
>   📁 Birthday
>
> Folder: ArtWorks
>
> [Make New Folder]   [Move]   [Cancel]

Copy of…

If you copy a file into the same folder, it will be renamed 'Copy of…' (the original filename).

RENAMING FILES

1 *If you want to edit or retype a file's name, select the file and press* **[F2]** *on your keyboard, or use* **Rename** *from the* **Organize menu** *or the right-click shortcut menu.*

2 *Change the name as required and press* **[Enter]** *to fix the new name.*

> Open
> Open in Same Window
> Print
> Open with   ▶
> Share with   ▶
> Restore previous versions
> Send to   ▶
> Cut
> Copy
> Create shortcut
> Delete
> Rename
> Open file location
> Properties

Extensions

When renaming files, do not change their extensions! If you do, you will lose the document–application link (page 136).

SENDING FILES ELSEWHERE

The **Send To** command on the **File menu** or on the shortcut menu offers a simple way to copy the selected file(s) to a compressed folder or a removable disk or to your Mail system for sending by e-mail. Just select the destination to begin.

Open	
Open in Same Window	
Print	
Open with ▶	
Share with ▶	
Restore previous versions	
Send to ▶	Compressed (zipped) folder
	Desktop (create shortcut)
Cut	Documents
Copy	Fax recipient
Create shortcut	Mail recipient
Delete	Skype
Rename	DVD RW Drive (D:)
Open file location	Removable Disk (H:)
Properties	

DELETING FILES

If a file is no longer needed, select it and press [**Delete**] on your keyboard or use the **File > Delete** command. If you delete a folder, all its files are also deleted.

Windows makes it very difficult to delete files by accident! First, you have to confirm – or cancel – the deletion at the prompt.

Second, nothing is permanently deleted at this stage. Instead, the file or folder is transferred to the Recycle Bin. Let's have a look at that now.

7.11 The Recycle Bin

The true value of the Recycle Bin is only fully appreciated by those of us who have used systems which lack this refinement, and have spent hours – or sometimes days – replacing files deleted in error! In practice, you will rarely need the Bin, but when you do, you will be glad that it is there!

If you find that you need a deleted file, it can be restored easily.

1 *Open the Recycle Bin, from the Desktop icon or in Windows Explorer (at the end of the Folders list).*
2 *Select the file(s).*
3 *Open the **File** menu, or right-click for the shortcut menu and select **Restore**, or click the **Restore this item** button.*
▶ *If the file's folder has also been deleted, it will be re-created first, so that the file can go back where it came from.*

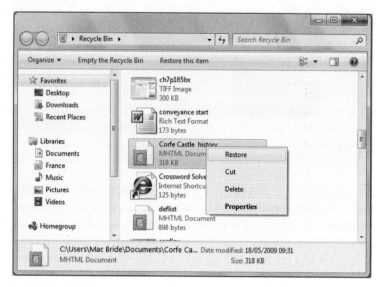

Figure 7.23 Files deleted in error can be restored from the Bin.

One of the main reasons for deleting files is to free up disk space, but as long as they are in the Recycle Bin, they are still on the disk. So, make a habit of emptying the Bin from time to time.

▶ *There is an* **Empty the Recycle Bin** *button on the toolbar, and an* **Empty...** *option on the* **File** *menu (when no files are selected). But only empty the Bin when you are absolutely sure that there is nothing in it that you might want to restore.*

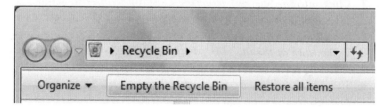

▶ *The default settings allow the Recycle Bin to use up to 10% of the drive's capacity, which should work well. If you want to change this, right-click on the Bin's icon to open its Properties panel and set the level there.*

Play safe!

Always open the Bin, check its contents and restore any accidental deletions, before you use the Empty Recycle Bin command.

7.12 Searching for files

Windows Explorer has a neat Search utility, which can track down lost files for you. If you organize your folders properly, and always store files in the right places, you'll never need this utility. However, if you are like me, you will appreciate it.

A search can be by all or part of the filename, or the content of text files (in indexed folders). Here's how to find a file if you can remember what it was called, or one of its tags, or a keyword in it, but not where you stored it.

1 *In the Navigation pane in Explorer, select the library or the highest level folder that it could be in. The search routine will go through any subfolders.*
2 *Click into the **Search** box and type all or part of the name or of a significant word in its text. Almost as soon you start to type, the search results will be displayed in the Contents Pane. Type more of the filename, the results will be filtered further, reducing the number of matching files.*

3 *Double-click on the file to open it, or make a note of its folder so that you can find it easily again later.*

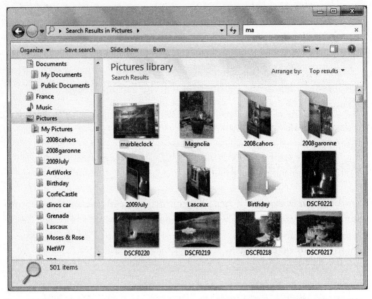

Figure 7.24 The results of search – if you get too many results, click back into the Search box and you will be able to filter them by Kind, Date, Type or Name.

THINGS TO REMEMBER

▶ Libraries and folders create organized storage for your files.

▶ Windows Explorer is the main utility for managing files and has a comprehensive set of tools.

▶ The View options allow you to set up the display to suit yourself.

▶ You should create folders for each area of your computer work. Folders can be created within other folders.

▶ Desktop shortcuts can be created by dragging file or folder icons from Explorer onto the Desktop.

▶ You can add tags to many types of files, and these can be used when sorting or searching for files.

▶ Files can be displayed in various views and can be sorted or filtered by name, size, type, tag, date or other properties.

▶ To create a file association, select the application when Windows asks you what it should open a document with.

▶ To select sets of files, drag an outline with the mouse, or use the mouse in combination with [Shift] or [Ctrl].

▶ Files can be moved, copied, renamed or deleted.

▶ When renaming files, do not change the extensions, as these identify the type of document.

▶ The Send command offers a simple way to e-mail a file to it to someone.

▶ When a file is deleted, it is transferred to the Recycle Bin. If necessary, files can be restored from the Bin.

▶ The Search routine offers a simple way to track down files.

SELF TEST

1 How do you know from the Title bar that a window is running Windows Explorer?

2 How can you change the way that files and folders are displayed?

3 When creating a folder, does it matter where you are?

4 How do you add a tag to a file? And why would you bother to add one?

5 Which keys are useful when selecting files?

6 What is a file extension?

7 How can you e-mail a file from within Windows Explorer?

8 What should you do if you delete a file then realize that you need it?

9 How would you start to find a file if you had forgotten where you had stored it?

8

Internet Explorer

8.1 What is the Internet?

This chapter concentrates on setting up and using Internet
Explorer. We will have a brief look at some of the facilities that
can be reached through the Internet, but there isn't room in this
book to tackle this huge area properly. If you want to know more
about the Internet, try *Teach Yourself The Internet*.

First of all, the Internet is *not* the World Wide Web – they are two
different, but intertwined things. The Internet is the hardware – the
computers and their connections – and the software that allows
them to communicate with each other. The Web is one way in
which information and services are shared over the Internet.

Over 50 million computers (and more every day) are permanently
connected to the Internet and offer services to its users. Some of
these *hosts* store information – text, pictures, sound or video files;
some hold programs that visitors can run; some are connections,
passing on messages between computers; some are servers at
service providers, allowing ordinary users – you and me – to
connect to the Internet and to store our Web pages. And when
you go online, your computer becomes part of the Internet.

The host computers are owned and managed by governments,
businesses, universities and other organizations. The connections
between them are a mixture of public and private telephone lines,
cables and microwave links. No single organization owns or

controls the Internet – about the nearest thing you have to central control are the agencies which allocate names to Web sites. It may sound a bit chaotic, but it works!

The Internet started as a 1960s US government project to develop a communications system that could survive a nuclear attack. Fortunately, it has never been tested in full(!) and just as fortunately it was allowed to expand. It spread first into military and research establishments within the USA and overseas, linking the networks in each organization into an *internetwork*. Some US universities set up their own internetwork links, and these joined into the Government's net in the mid-1980s to form the core of the Internet. Since then, it has expanded enormously, so that now almost all of the world's universities and schools, all big businesses and most smaller ones, most governments and political parties, pressure groups and charities, are online.

The important thing is that the Internet was not set up as a commercial venture. Even today, when many businesses are advertising and selling goods and services on the Internet, a large part of it remains non-commercial. Much of the data that flows across the Net is generated by people having fun – sharing ideas and tracking down information on their enthusiasms, keeping in touch with remote friends, old and new, playing games, or just plain 'surfing' to see what they can find.

8.2 Getting online

Windows 7 PCs are usually Internet-ready. Most new laptops are Wi-Fi enabled, i.e. they have a built-in wireless broadband modem and the necessary software so that they can connect to any available wireless network. Desktop PCs do not usually have a built-in modem, but that's because the manufacturers expect you to sign up for a broadband connection, and the ISP (Internet Service Provider) will supply the modem.

Exactly how you set up a connection depends upon which ISP you use, but it will normally be very straightforward – there will be an installation CD and a booklet. Follow the instructions, and you should be up and running and online within minutes.

If broadband is not available where you live, you will have to use a dial-up account, and you will need a standard modem. This should cost you around £50 and is easily added – just plug it into a spare USB port. Your dial-up provider should supply you with an installation CD, but if they don't, Windows 7 has a wizard that will help you set up your end of the connection – look in the Connect to the Internet area of the Welcome Center.

8.3 Internet Explorer

You can access the Internet from many places in the Windows 7 system, but the main tool for this job is Internet Explorer

The online Desktop?

Microsoft would like you to view the Internet as an extension of your Desktop. If you connect through an always-on broadband line, then this is a viable view. If you connect by dialling in to a service provider, the transition from Desktop to Internet will rarely be smooth or swift.

Internet Explorer is designed for fast, easy navigation, both on and offline. When you browse a page, its files are stored in a temporary folder on your hard disk. When you return to the same page, its files are then loaded from the disk, rather than down-loaded from the Internet. This can make browsing far quicker, as you often find that you want to go back and have another look at a page, to read it more closely or to pick up new leads.

THE INTERNET EXPLORER WINDOW

▶ *The* **Address bar** *shows you where you are. You can type an address here to go to a Web page. At the end of the bar:*
▶ ⟳ *Refresh will reload the current page – click this if the page stalls when loading in.*

▶ 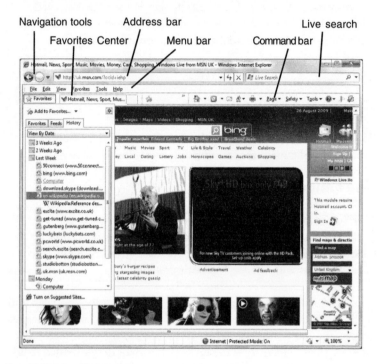 Stop – click this when you realize at the start of a long download that you don't really want to see that page.

▶ The **Menu bar** is optional – the tools can all be reached through the Command bar.

▶ The **Favorites Center** can display Favorites or History (page 168) or Feeds (see below).

Navigation tools   Address bar   Live search

Favorites Center   Menu bar   Command bar

Figure 8.1 The Internet Explorer window.

The navigation tools

Figure 8.2 The navigation tools.

Use these to move between the pages you have already visited during the session:

▶ **Back** *takes you to the page you have just left.*
▶ **Forward** *reverses the Back movement.*
▶ *The drop-down page list allows you to select from the last dozen or so pages.*

The Command bar

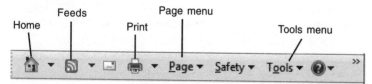

Figure 8.3 The Command bar tools – there are a few more, less-used, tools which you can see by clicking the double-chevron on the right.

These buttons contain almost all of the controls that you need when you are online.

▶ **Home** *goes to your start page – your jumping off point into the Web. This can be your own home page or any other.*

▶ **Feeds** *are used to alert you to new content in Web pages. Not all sites offer a feeds service – click the button when you are on a page to see if feeds are available from it.*

▶ **Read mail** *opens your e-mail application.*

▶ **Print** *prints the current page (text and graphics).*

The Page menu

The commands here are largely concerned with the content of pages. These are worth noting:

▶ **Copy** *copies text or images for pasting into a document.*

▶ **Save As** *stores a copy of the page (see page 171).*

▶ **Zoom** *enlarges the text and graphics.*

▶ **Text size** *enlarges, or reduces, the text size.*

The Safety menu

The commands on this menu relate to safety and privacy online. These are worth knowing about:

▶ **Delete Browsing History** *opens a dialog box where you can delete the records of your visits and the temporary files that Explorer stores to speed up displays if you revisit. Use this to free up disk space if you are running low.*

▶ **In-Private Browsing** *opens a new window where you can browse without anything being recorded in the History or the Address bar (see page 167).*

154

- **In-Private Filtering** *can be used to block content on web pages if that content collects information on your browsing habits. This data can be used to create targeted adverts.*
- **SmartScreen Filter** *helps to protect your PC from malicious websites. This should be turned on.*

The Tools menu
The key commands to note here are:

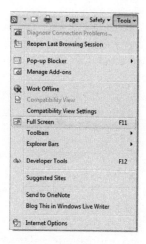

- **Pop-up Blocker:** *turn this on to block pop-up windows – usually carrying adverts – opening when you visit Web pages.*
- **Full screen** *removes the toolbars and uses the entire screen to display a page.*
- *The* **Toolbars** *submenu controls the display of toolbars and sidebars.*
- **Internet Options** *allow you to configure Explorer to suit your needs.*

8.4 Internet Options

These options can be set or changed at any time online or offline (though some only take effect after you restart the PC). A few should be set before you start to use Explorer in earnest, others are best left until you have been using it for a while and have a clearer idea of what settings best suit the way you like to work.

- *Use* **Tools > Internet Options** *to open the panel, and click on the tab names to move between the sets of options.*
- *If you set options that change the appearance, click* **Apply** *to see how they look.*
- *Only click* **OK** *when you have finished with all the tabs.*

The Home page defines where Internet Explorer goes when it is started. This could be a personalized start page at your Internet access provider site (or elsewhere – many sites offer this facility), your own home page, or a blank page if each session is a new voyage. An address can be typed in here, but it is simpler to wait until you are online at the right place, then come to here and click **Use Current**.

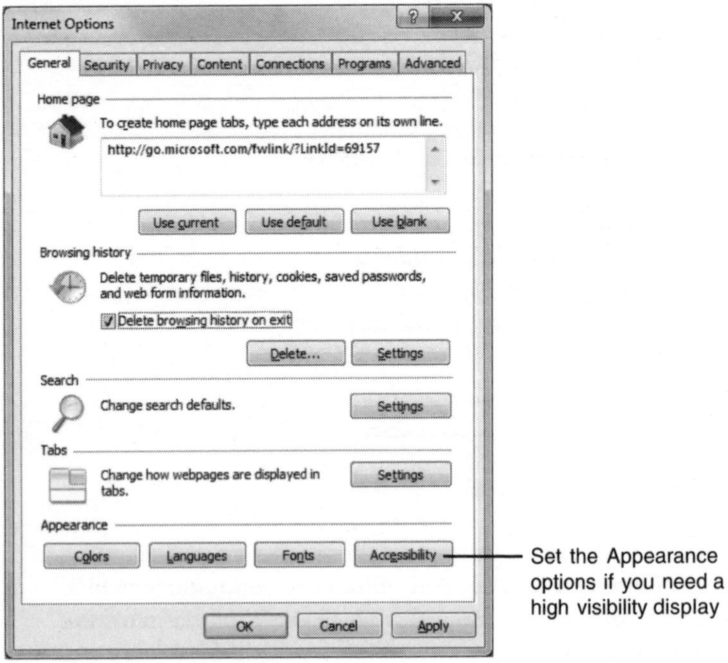

Set the Appearance options if you need a high visibility display

Figure 8.4 Setting the General options.

Can you see it clearly?

Some web pages are not designed with accessibility in mind. If you need to keep a high visibility display, click the Accessibility button on the General tab and turn on the options to ignore the colours and fonts specified in web pages.

In **Browsing History,** click **Settings** to define how Explorer should handle page files.

▶ *In the* **Check for newer version of stored pages,** *select* **Every time I visit the webpage,** *if the pages you use most change frequently.*

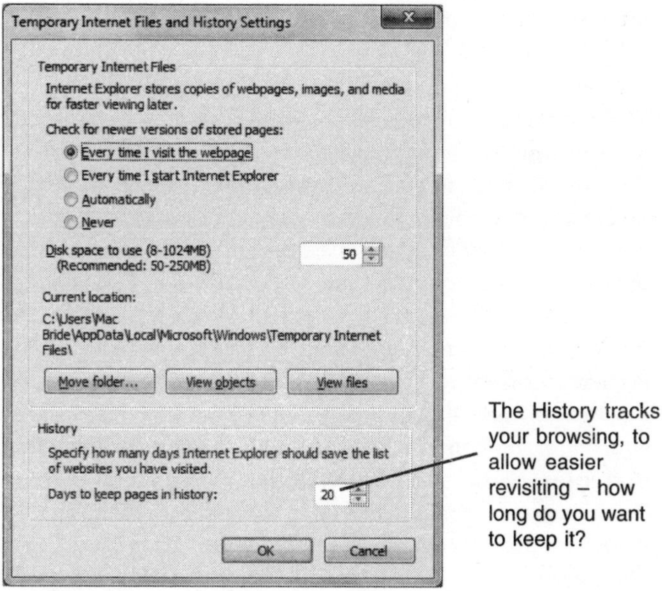

Figure 8.5 The History Settings. The History tracks your browsing, to allow easier revisiting – how long do you want to keep it?

The History tracks your browsing, to allow easier revisiting – how long do you want to keep it?

▶ *The Amount of* **Disk space to use** *depends upon how much browsing you do, how often you return to pages, how long you like to keep pages in your History and how much space you have. As a general rule, allocate as much space as you can easily spare and see how it goes.*

In **Search** you can change to a different search engine from the default Live Search – but give this a try first, it's good!

In **Tabs** you can define how and where new pages open – in tabs or windows. Come back to this after you have spent more time online.

SECURITY AND PRIVACY

The Internet is basically a safe place – as long as you take a few sensible precautions. If you spend most of your time at major commercial and other well-established sites, and at ones they recommend, security should not be a major concern. If you browse more widely, you may bump up against the mischievous and the unscrupulous. The main problems are these:

▶ **Viruses** – *You can only get these by running programs or macros in documents. You cannot pick up a virus simply by browsing a page or reading e-mail or news articles. A virus-checker will give you an extra level of protection.*

▶ **Active content** – *Web designers may use small programs (applets), written in Java, Javascript or ActiveX to enhance their pages – though many are just decorative. The languages are designed to be secure – the programs should not be able to access your system – but hackers do find loopholes.*

▶ **Privacy intrusions** – *Every time you fill in a form online, run a search or make a choice, you send some information about yourself along with the intended data. Some sites may attempt to store and misuse this information.*

▶ **Cookies** – *A cookie is a short file, written by a site onto your hard disk. They are normally used to store your preferences at that site – so that when you revisit you don't have to set preferences again – or to log your visit. There are different sorts of cookies, some more intrusive than others. On the* **Privacy** *tab, you can set your limits for accepting cookies.*

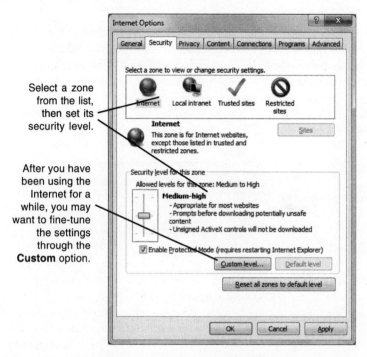

Select a zone from the list, then set its security level.

After you have been using the Internet for a while, you may want to fine-tune the settings through the **Custom** option.

Figure 8.6 The Security tab – when in doubt, play safe! IE sorts sites into four zones: Local intranet, Trusted sites, Restricted sites and Internet (everything else). At first leave the default levels or nudge them a little higher. To do this, select a zone from the list, then click the slider to set its security level.

Custom settings

When you are more aware of what you are likely to meet and how you like to use the Internet, you may like to use the Custom Level to define how IE is to respond to sites in each zone.

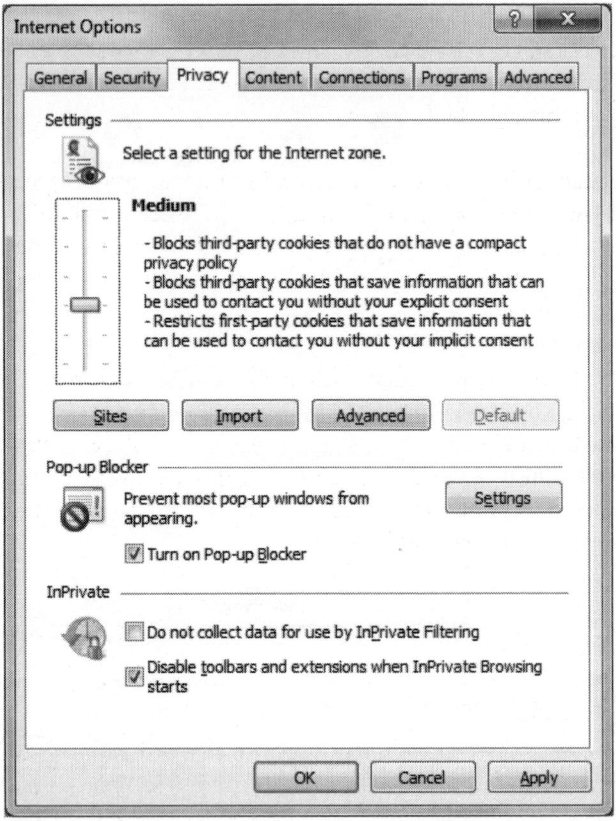

Figure 8.7 Using the Privacy tab to control cookies. The more you block, the safer you are, but some sites will not let you in if you block cookies. The Advanced options allow you to set up IE so that you can decide whether or not to accept cookies which would otherwise be blocked.

Certificates

Certificates guarantee that people and sites are who they say they are. You can get one for yourself as an ID to use with your mail and at some sites. A Publisher's certificate shows you can trust the site.

CONTENT ADVISOR AND SAFE SURFING

If children can get online from your PC, you may want to enable the Content Advisor to set limits to the types of material that they can access through the Internet.

The Content Advisor allows you to restrict unsupervised access to those sites which have been rated by the Recreational Software Advisory Council for the Internet (RASCi). This rates sites on a scale of 1 to 5 for language, nudity, sex and violence. You set the limits of what may be accessed from your machine.

Many perfectly acceptable sites do not have a rating, simply because they have not applied for one, but this is not a major problem. It just means that the kids will have to ask someone who knows the password to override the restrictions when they find somewhere good but unrated. And if you want to browse unrestricted, you can disable the advisor.

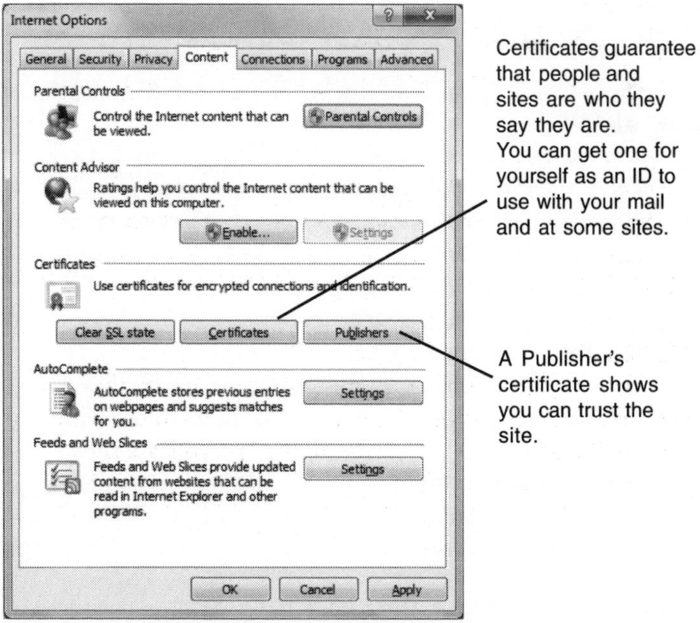

Certificates guarantee that people and sites are who they say they are.
You can get one for yourself as an ID to use with your mail and at some sites.

A Publisher's certificate shows you can trust the site.

Figure 8.8 The Content tab. Turn on Content Advisor if you are going to let children have unsupervised access to the Internet. The Parental Controls button links to the standard Parental Controls (page 227).

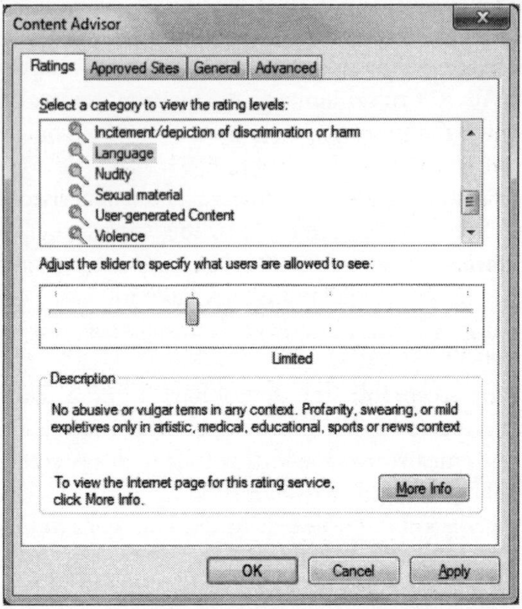

Figure 8.9 Defining what is acceptable. Note that these limits only apply to rated sites, and the majority of sites are unrated. On the General tab you can allow access to unrated sites, or supervised access to rated sites.

Safer surfing

If you are concerned about people reaching the murkier corners of the Internet, Content Advisor is only the first line of defence. For more about child safety, try these sites:

www.safekids.com
www.child-internet-safety.com
www.childnet-int.org

ADVANCED

Most of the **Advanced** options should be left well alone until you really know what you are doing, but there are a couple that you might want to look at now.

In the **Accessibility** section, **Always expand ALT text for images** will make sure that there is enough space to display all the ALT text if **Show Pictures** has been turned off.

At the bottom of the **Browsing** section, turn on **Use inline AutoComplete** if you want IE to try to finish URLs for you when you start typing them into the Address bar – this is a very handy facility.

In the **Multimedia** section, turn off the **Play** options for faster browsing.

8.5 Browsing the Web

Hyperlinks – addresses attached to text or images – provide an efficient means of following leads from page to page, but with so much information spread over so many pages on so many sites over the Web, the problem is where to start looking.

Your Internet Service Provider's home site will probably offer a directory with an organized set of links to selected sites, and Internet Explorer is initially set up to head to MSN (MicroSoft Network). This has a good directory, so you may as well leave it as your start point until you have found a better place, then change to its address in the Internet Options dialog box (page 155).

A directory is good for starting research on general topics, but if you are looking for specific material, you are probably better off running a search, and with Internet Explorer you can run a search at any time, no matter where you are on the Web.

RUNNING A SEARCH

1 *In the* **Live Search** *box at the top right of the IE window, type a word or phrase to describe what you are looking for.*
2 *As soon as you start to type, IE will give you a list of previous searches, or of suggested words that start with the same letters. This will change with each letter you type. If you can see what you want, click on it. If not, keep on typing.*
3 *Press* [Enter].
4 *When you get the results, click on a link to view the page.*

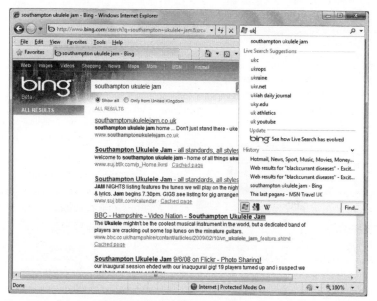

Figure 8.11 A search started in Internet Explorer is run at Live Search (though you can change to the search engine if you like). You are taken to the site for the results, and once there you can define your searches more closely, by selecting the types of results or by setting advanced options.

Other start points

There are many places that you can use as start points for your surfing. Some that are well worth a visit include:

Yahoo!'s main site – the original and probably still the best of the directories, at http://www.yahoo.com
Yahoo! UK & Ireland, at http://uk.yahoo.com
Excite offers an excellent directory, search and more, at http://www.excite.co.uk
The most comprehensive search engine is Google at http://www.google.com

But before you can get to these, you need to know about URLs. Read on!

Figure 8.12 There are local Yahoo!s in many countries, backed up by the central directory at www.yahoo.com. Yahoo! also offers web e-mail, news, weather, shopping and auctions, games, and more.

UNIFORM RESOURCE LOCATORS (URL)

With all the millions of web pages, files and other resources that can be reached over the Internet, a standardized way of identifying them is essential. URLs provide this. There are different styles of URL for each approach to the Internet, though they all follow much the same pattern:

type://hostcomputer/directory/filename

Web pages

Many of these are instantly recognizable from their html or htm endings, which shows that they are hypertext pages.

http://sunsite.unc.edu/boutell/faq/www-faq.html

This one is a list of frequently asked questions (faq) and their answers, about the World Wide Web (www), stored in the Sun archives in the University of North Carolina (unc).

The URL of the top page of a site may just consist of the site address, with an (optional) slash at the end. This is the opening page at Microsoft's site:

http://www.microsoft.com/

If you know the URL of a page, you can jump directly to it. Use **File > Open,** and type the URL into the panel, or type it into the **Address** toolbar.

The leading http:// is not really necessary. The browser expects you to enter a World Wide Web URL. Thus:

http://uk.yahoo.com

can be entered as:

uk.yahoo.com

URLs must be typed exactly right or they will not work. They are not usually case-sensitive (though a few are) but do watch out for symbols. Where a URL is to the top page of a site, it may end in a slash (/). This can be omitted.

HISTORY

When you want to return to a page, the simplest way is through the Back button and the list that drops down from it. This only works with those visited very recently – the Back list is wiped at the end of a session, and can be corrupted by movements within sites, especially those with complex, interactive page layouts. The most reliable way to revisit pages is by opening the History list in the Favorites Center – click the **History tab** to bring it to the front. The pages are grouped by day and then by site, making it easy to find the one you want.

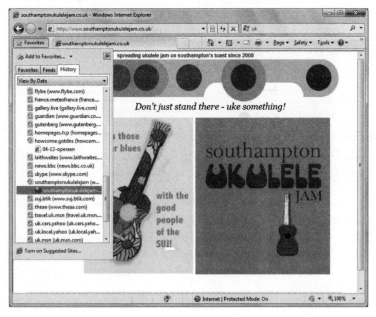

Figure 8.13 Using the History list. Pages are grouped into their sites.

FAVORITES

The Favorites Center can also display the Favorites list. This comes with a few sets of ready-made links, but is really intended as a store of links to places that you like to revisit regularly.

1 *When you find a page that you will want again in future, open the* **Favorites Center** *and click* **Add to Favorites.**
2 *Edit the name, if necessary – the page's title will be suggested.*
3 *If you want to store the link in a folder, open the* **Create in:** *list and choose it – a new folder can be created, if needed.*
4 *Click* **Add.**

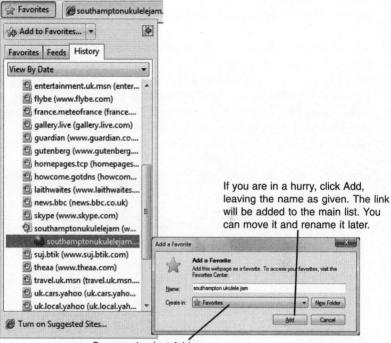

If you are in a hurry, click Add, leaving the name as given. The link will be added to the main list. You can move it and rename it later.

Open and select folders

Figure 8.14 Adding a page to the Favorites. If you are in a hurry, click Add, leaving the name as given. The link will be added to the main list. You can move it and rename it later. Otherwise, click the Create in button and select the Favorites folder to store it in.

Get organized!

If – more likely when – your Favorites folders get crowded and messy, click the arrow beside the Add to Favorites and select Organize Favorites to open a display of the folders. You can then move, rename, delete and generally sort out your stored links.

8.6 Files from the Net

SHAREWARE SITES

The Internet is a great source of software – particularly for software that you can use on the Internet – but it's also a great source games, music, videos, pictures, text files and more.

If you are looking for shareware, try these excellent sites, both run by clnet – shareware.com (http://www.shareware.com) and download. com (http://www.download.com). Here you can search by keyword or program, or browse by category. When you find something that you want, clicking on the program's name will start the download – decide which folder to store it in, and sit back and wait. On a broadband connection, you should be able to download 2MB or more in a minute.

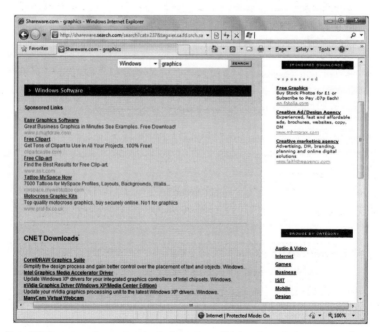

Figure 8.15 shareware.com – a great source of software. Some of it is free, the rest is shareware – try it for free, but pay to continue using it.

ZIPped files

Many of the files available online are compressed to save space. This reduces file sizes, and transfer times, by up to 90%. Zipped files can be opened in Windows Explorer.

SAVING WEB PAGES

You can revisit a page, offline, for as long as it is kept in the temporary files area, but if you want a permanent copy of a page you should save it.

▶ *Wait until the page is fully loaded, then open the* **Page** *menu and select* **Save As** – *you may need to change the filename to something memorable. The default Save As type is Web Archive, which packs the page, its images and any other components into a single file. This is a very compact way to store pages, but if you want to be able to look at the text and images separately, set the* **Save as type** *to* **Web Page complete**. *This will store any images and other files in a folder with the same name as the page.*

▶ *When you want to view the page again, use* **File > Open**, *then browse through your folders to locate it. The default store is Downloads – and that is as good a place as any.*

Figure 8.16 Saving a web page. If you just want the text of a simple page (but with its formatting and layout), set the Save as type to 'Webpage, HTML only'.

SAVING TEXT

The text of a Web page can be saved in two ways.

▶ *If you want all of the text on the page, use* **Page > Save As,** *and set the type to Text File.*
▶ *To save a chunk of the text, select it, use* **Page > Copy,** *and paste it into a word processor, then save it from there.*

SAVING IMAGES

If you don't want the whole page, but just an individual image from it, this can be saved separately.

▶ *Point anywhere on the picture and wait for the image toolbar to appear, then click the* **Save this image** *button.*
▶ *If you really like the image and it is big enough to make a good background for your Desktop, right-click on it and select* **Set as background** *from the short menu.*

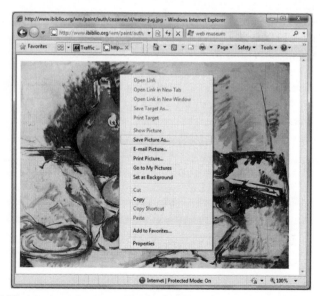

Figure 8.17 Saving an image off a web page. This is from the Web Museum which has good quality images of many great paintings – you could download one and set it as the background to the Desktop. You can view the Museum at many sites, including http://www.southern.net/wm

8.7 Windows Live

Microsoft offers a set of programs – Windows Live Essentials – for free download. They are not all actually 'essential', but some are certainly useful. What they have in common is that they all, to a greater or lesser extent, make use of the Internet for sharing and exchanging text, images or other files with other people.

The programs are:

▶ **Messenger** – *for real-time exchange of messages and images with other Messenger users.*
▶ **Mail** – *a fully equipped e-mail program. You will need this and we will be looking at it in the next chapter.*
▶ **Writer** – *for creating and uploading text and images to blogging sites.*
▶ **Photo Gallery** – *for organizing, editing, printing and otherwise working with your digital photos. This is very useful, as you will see in Chapter 12.*
▶ **Movie Maker** – *for editing and publishing home videos.*
▶ **Family Safety** – *filters and other controls to restrict how children can use the PC and what they can access on the Internet.*
▶ **Toolbar** – *an add-on to Internet Explorer giving quick links to the Windows Live facilities.*

The programs can only be downloaded as a set – but you do not have to install them all. To get the Live package:

1 *Click the* **Start** *button.*
2 *Click the arrow to the right of* **Getting Started,** *and on its submenu select* **Get Windows Live Essentials.**

3 *When you get to the Windows Live site, click the* **Download** *button.*

4 *At the* **File Download** *dialog box, click* **Run.** *What you are getting at this point is just a control program, which is quite small.*

5 *When the file is downloaded it will start to run automatically, and the* **User Account Control** *dialog box will check that you mean to run this. You do!*

6 *The main download is over 130Mb and will take a few minutes. Once it comes in, the Live software will begin to install.*

92% of wlsetup-all.exe from download.microsof...

wlsetup-all.exe from download.microsoft.com

Estimated time left: 55 sec (122MB of 133MB copied)
Download to: Temporary Folder
Transfer rate: 205KB/Sec

☐ Close this dialog box when download completes

Open | Open Folder | Cancel

SmartScreen Filter checked this download and did not report any threats. Report an unsafe download.

7 *You will be shown a service agreement – accept it.*

8 *Select the programs that you want to install.*

Windows Live

Choose the programs you want to install

Click each program name for details.

- ☐ Microsoft Office Live Ad...
- ☐ Messenger
- ☐ Mail
- ☐ Photo Gallery
- ☐ Toolbar
- ☐ Writer
- ☐ Family Safety
- ☐ Movie Maker Beta

Mail

With Windows Live Mail on your desktop, you can access multiple e-mail accounts in one program, plus your calendar, newsgroups, and feeds. And it's part of Windows Live, so you can view your calendar online, and see when Messenger contacts are available to chat.

Installed with this program:

- Microsoft Application Error Reporting
- Microsoft Visual Studio Runtime
- Windows Live Communications Platform
- Junk Mail filter update

Space needed: 175 MB
Space available: 186 GB

[Install] [Cancel]

9 *Click Install, and wait – installation takes a while.*
10 *When the installation has finished, you will find a new folder on your Start menu – click* **All Programs**, *then click* **Windows Live** *to start exploring your new programs.*

WINDOWS UPDATE

Windows 7 comes with an automatic update system. This will
check the Microsoft website regularly, when you are online, to see
if there are updates available that you should have. If there are, the

system will download and install them for you. You don't need to do anything about this – it just happens!

> ▶ *If you prefer to control when and how your Windows 7 software is updated, you can turn this facility off – open* **Automatic Updates** *in the Control Panel and switch to manual control.*

If you choose to update manually, or want to see what optional updates are available, click on the **Windows Update** shortcut on the main **Start** menu. This is a highly automated page. It has routines that will check over your system to see if there are any files for which new replacements or 'patch' repairs are available. If there are any – or if you find any optional add-ons that you would like – they will be downloaded and installed for you.

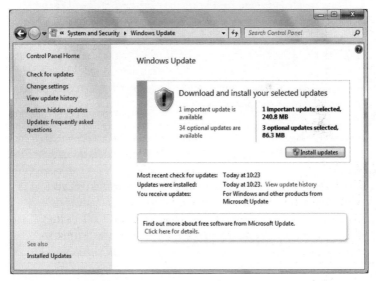

Figure 8.18 The Windows Update page.

THINGS TO REMEMBER

▶ *The Internet is the result of world-wide cooperation between computer networks in commercial, educational and other organizations.*

▶ *Getting online is simple with Windows 7, especially with a broadband connection.*

▶ *Some of the Internet options should be set early on; others can be left until you have spent more time online.*

▶ *If children can get online from your PC, you should enable the Content Advisor.*

▶ *Directories help you find your way around; Yahoo! is the most comprehensive of these. Search engines can be used to track down pages containing keywords. You can also search from the Live Search box in Explorer.*

▶ *The Web consists of pages linked together by URLs given as hyperlinks in the pages.*

▶ *Every site on the Internet has its own unique address. If you know the URL of a page, you can jump directly to it.*

▶ *The Favorites Center can be used to display the History or Favorites shortcuts.*

▶ *Files can be downloaded from many places on the Net – shareware sites hold stores of free and cheap software.*

▶ *A Web page can be saved as a file. Text and pictures can also be saved separately.*

▶ *Download and install (some of) the Live Essentials programs.*

▶ *Use Windows Update to keep your system up to date.*

SELF TEST

1   *Are the Internet and the World Wide Web two names for the same thing?*

2   *How would you start to change the Internet Explorer display and/or the way it works?*

3   *What two features allow you to control your children's access to the World Wide Web?*

4   *What is a search engine? Which is the leading search engine?*

5   *What does a hyperlink do?*

6   *Why is it useful to know the address of a website?*

7   *What is a Favorite?*

8   *How can you save the text and images of a web a page on your PC?*

9   *Why should you get Live Essentials?*

10 *What does Windows Update do?*

9

....

Live Mail

9.1 Live Mail

Windows Live Mail is part of the Live Essentials package that we
looked at in Chapter 8. It is an e-mail program, which is all we
are using it for here, though it does have some additional features.
It can be used to access feeds (which we met in Chapter 6) and
newsgroups and is linked with the Calendar (neither of which do
we have room to cover here),

Newsgroups

Newsgroups were once the main way in which people came
together online to share interests and enthusiasms. They were
where you could ask for and give help, debate and announce
new discoveries and ideas. At the peak there were over
50,000 each devoted to a different topic, from the seriously
academic to the totally trivial. Newsgroups still exist, and
some have large and active memberships, but their role has
largely been replaced by blogs and chat rooms. Dip into them
sometime, to see if there is anything there for you.

Live Mail can be started from the **Start** menu. The first few times
you will have to go into All Programs and open the Windows Live
folder to get it, but with regular use it will soon become part of the
initial display.

The default layout of the Live Mail window has the Folder pane on the left, the Reading pane with the Message list above it on the right, and the toolbar across the top. The display can be customized through the Layout routine – reach this through the Menus button or the **View menu**.

- The **Folder pane** *shows the folders in which messages are stored, and is used for navigating between them.*
- The **Message list** *shows the essential details of the messages in the selected folder.*
- The **Reading pane** *displays the message selected in the Header Pane.*
- The **Toolbar** *gives you quick access to the most used commands.*
- The **Menu bar** *is normally hidden, but can be turned on – permanently, or as needed.*

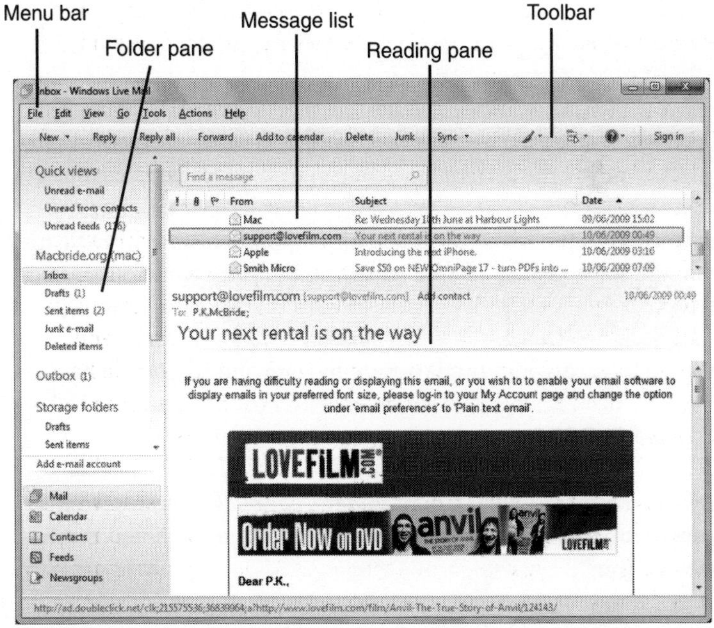

Figure 9.1 The Windows Mail screen. The View > Columns... option lets you select which items to display in the headers, but from, subject and received are generally enough to be able to find and sort messages.

The Menu bar

If you want to use the keyboard to select commands, turn on the Menu bar from the Menus button, or press [Alt] to make the Menu bar appear whenever you need it.

THE TOOLBAR

New ▾   Reply   Reply all   Forward   Add to calendar   Delete   Junk   Sync ▾   ✎ ▾   📑 ▾   ❓ ▾   Sign in

The toolbar buttons, left to right:

New – click to start a new message.

Reply – starts a message to the sender of the selected message.

Reply All – sends the message to everyone who got copies of the original message.

Forward – sends a message on to another person.

Add to Calendar – adds the date of a meeting to the Calendar

Delete – moves the selected message(s) to the Deleted Items folder

Junk – marks the message as unwanted junk mail. Any future mail from the same sender will be moved to the Junk folder as soon as it arrives.

Sync – Links to your e-mail service to send and receive messages.

THE FOLDERS

At first, there are only six mail folders. More can be created to provide organized storage for any mail messages and newsgroups that you join.

▶ *The* **Inbox** *holds mail sent to you. The messages remain here, after reading, until you move or delete them.*

184

- *The **Outbox** provides temporary storage for messages, while they are waiting to be sent. If you have a dial-up line, and pay by the minute for access, it makes sense to compose your messages offline, and only go online to send them and collect incoming mail.*
- *The **Sent** folder keeps a copy of outgoing messages, if you choose to keep copies (see page 191).*
- **Deleted Items** *is where messages and articles are stored when they are first deleted. They are only removed completely when deleted from here.*
- *Use **Drafts** as a temporary store for messages that you want to work on some more before sending.*
- **Junk E-mail** *is where Live Mail puts those incoming messages which it thinks are junk. If you have a good ISP, and if you don't publish your e-mail address – tell it to your friends, but not to the world – then you shouldn't get too much junk.*

Creating folders

If you need to keep messages for future reference, it is a good idea to set up a new folder for each project, or person. Creating a folder is simple. Click on the mail account (the name above the Inbox), then click the arrow on the **New** button and select **Folder** from the menu. Give the new folder a suitable name, and you are done.

9.2 Reading mail

Start by selecting the Inbox folder – if it is not already selected – to display its message headers. These show the name of the sender, the subject and when the message was received. They are normally in date order, but can be sorted by sender, subject or date, by clicking on the column name. If the message has not yet been read, its header will be in **bold**. When you select a header, the message is displayed in the preview pane (or in a separate window, if you have chosen this option).

When a message is displayed, these tools are available for dealing with it:

▶ **Reply** – *opens the New Message window, with the sender's name in the To: slot, ready to send back to them. This is neat as it means that you do not have to think about their e-mail address.*

▶ **Reply to all** – *use this instead of Reply where a message has been mailed to a group of people, and you want your reply to reach the whole group! Your reply will then be mailed to all those who received a To: or Cc: copy (page 188) of the message.*

▶ **Forward** – *copies the message into the New Message window, so that you can send it on to another person. This time you will have to supply the address, just as if you were sending a new message – see below.*

▶ **Delete** – *moves the message to the Deleted folder. You can get Live Mail to empty the Deleted folder for you on exit, or let them stay there, where they can be recovered if necessary – as with the Recycle Bin – until you delete them from there.*

▶ *You can also drag a message, at any time, from the header list to another folder for storage.*

When people send you mail, it is stored in your mailbox at your Internet service provider.

If you have an always-on broadband connection, you can set up the options (page 190), so that Windows Mail checks the box and downloads new messages for you at set intervals.

If you have a dial-up connection, you can go online to pick up mail, and send messages in the Outbox, whenever it suits you. Click the **Sync** button to send and receive your mail and to pick up any new feeds, or drop down its list and select your mail account if you only want to deal with your mail.

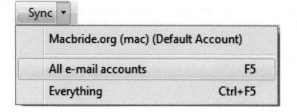

Clear out the junk!

Obviously, you will delete junk mail as soon as it comes in – but don't stop there. After you have read a message – and responded to it if necessary – then delete it unless you need to keep it for future reference. Don't let your Inbox get cluttered with old, unwanted messages.

9.3 Sending mail

Live Mail, like most modern mail software, can handle messages in HTML format (as used on Web pages), as well as plain text. This means that you can use different fonts, sizes and colours for your text, set bulleted or numbered lists and other layout options, and insert pictures. If you want colourful messages, without the bother of formatting them, there are a dozen Stationery styles. These give you decorative backgrounds and some also have matching text formats already set.

To write and send a message:

1 *Click the* **New** *button, or use the command* **File > New > E-mail Message**.

Or

2 *When the New Message window opens, if you want a decorated background for your message, click the* **Stationery** *button and pick one from the list, or select* **More Stationery** *to see the whole range. (The list starts off empty, but each one you use is added to it.)*

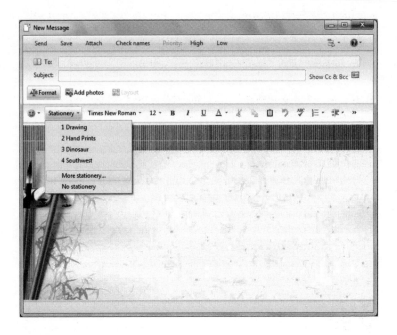

3 *Type the recipient's e-mail address into the* **To:** *box, or click* **To:** *and select it from your Contacts list (see page 195 for more on Contacts).*

4 *If more than one person is to get a copy, add addresses in the* **To:** *box (separated by semicolons or commas), or click the* **Show Cc: & Bcc:** *link to open those boxes and add the addresses there.*

To: the main recipients – you would normally expect to get replies from these people.

Cc: Carbon copies, sent mainly for information.

Bcc: Blind carbon copies – their names will not appear in the lists of recipients that normally accompany each message. Used for circulating mail to large groups.

5 *Type a* **Subject** *for the message, so that the recipients know what it is about when they see the header.*

6 *Type and format your message. If you don't have the spell checker set to run automatically, you should read the message through to check for errors.*

7 *Click the* **Send** *button. If the spell checker is turned on, it will now run. After you have worked through any errors it finds, the message will be sent immediately, or stored in the Outbox to be sent later – it depends on the settings (see below).*

Or

8 *If you want to override your default send settings, open the* **File** *menu and select* **Send Message** *(i.e. now) or* **Send Later**.

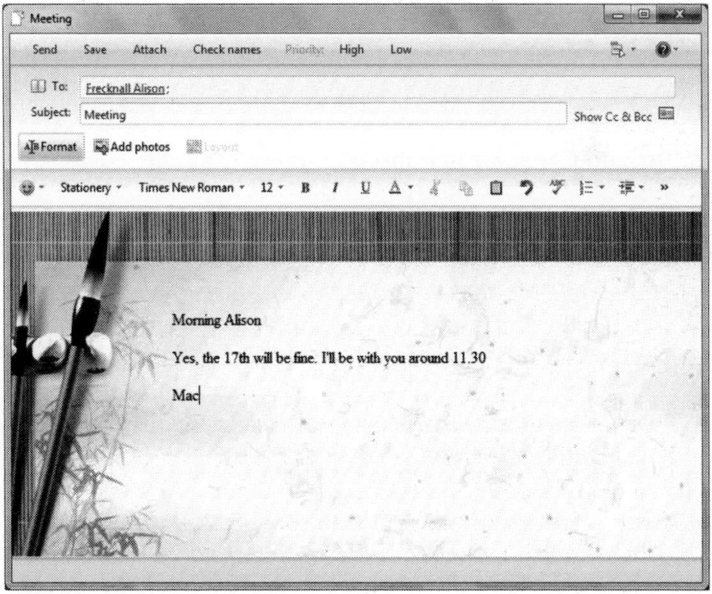

Figure 9.2 Composing a message using the Drawing stationery – apply formats as in normal word-processing.

No time to finish?

If you haven't finished writing a message, but run out of time, click the Save button. The message will be saved in the Drafts folder. When you want to carry on, double-click on the message to reopen it, complete it and send as normal.

9.4 Live Mail options

As with most software, the optional settings make more sense after you have been using it for a while, and the defaults are usually a safe bet to start with. However, there are a few that are worth checking and setting early on. Click the **Menus** button and select **Options...** to open the **Options** panel.

The **General** tab deals with the interaction between Live Mail and your system.

▶ Turn on **Check for new messages every ?? minutes**, *and set the interval, if you are always online.*
▶ *Turn off* **Notify me if there are any new newsgroups** *if you don't bother with the news.*
▶ *All the other options are probably best turned on at this stage.*

The **Read** tab is mainly concerned with news articles.

▶ *Some groups have hundreds of articles every day. You can set how many headers to download at a time.*

The **Receipts** tab set how to deal with receipts. You can request them when sending messages, and people may ask you for them.

The **Send** tab is mainly about message formats (see Figure 9.3).

▶ *Turn on* **Save copy of sent messages** *only if you normally need to keep a copy for later reference.*
▶ *Turn on* **Send messages immediately** *if you normally deal with your mail online.*
▶ *Turning on* **Automatically put people I reply to in my address book after the third reply** *is a very neat idea. It ensures that their address is correct – but as it only does this for people that you are likely to be in regular contact with.*

▶ *The* **Include message in reply** *option can be useful, especially if most of your e-mail is work-related. When replying, you can edit out any unwanted bits of the original message.*

▶ *Set your* **Mail Sending Format** *to* **HTML** *if most of your recipients are able to read HTML-formatted messages.*

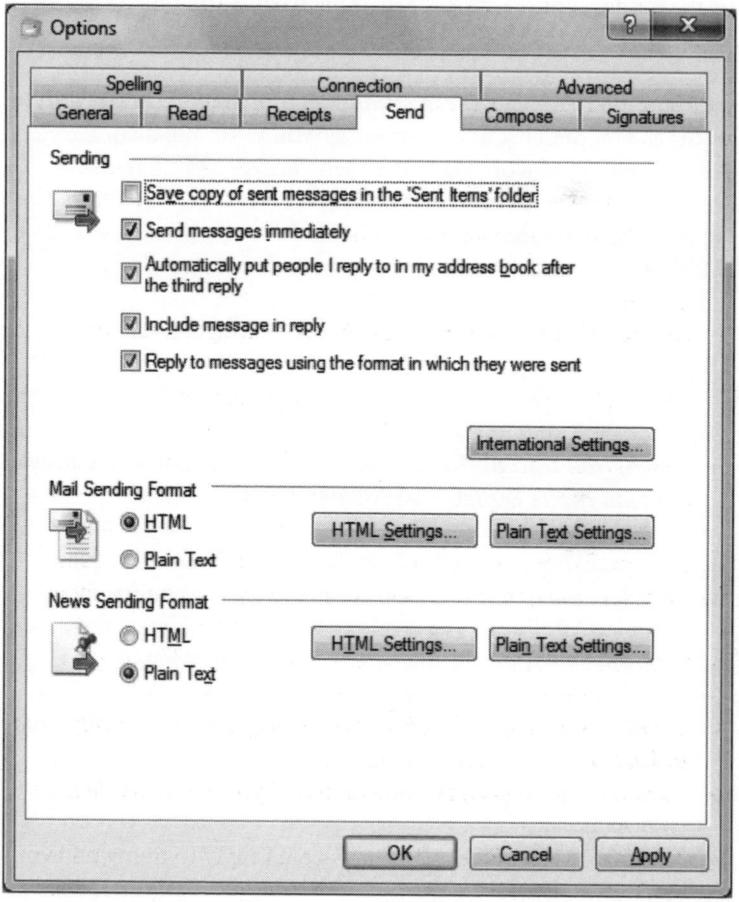

Figure 9.3 The Send options.

The **Compose** tab lets you define your message format, setting the default fonts and stationery.

Signatures are short files that can be attached to the end of every message. People use them to add their other contact details, or – in companies – to carry disclaimers that the views expressed are those of the sender, not the firm. They are entirely optional.

The **Spelling** tab controls the way that the spell checker works. The main option is *Always check spelling before sending* – turn this on or off as you prefer. Other options let you select the dictionary and define the kind of words that the spell checker should ignore.

The **Connection** tab controls when and how you go online and off again. If things are working nicely, leave this alone.

The **Advanced** tab options can be left at their defaults, but click the Maintenance button and set how to clean up messages.

▶ *Turn on* **Empty messages from the Deleted Items folder on exit** *unless you tend to delete items in error. If this is off, you will have to delete the messages again to remove them.*
▶ *Compacting the database does not delete messages, but stores them more efficiently.*
▶ *The remaining options refer to newsgroup messages. How long – if at all – do you want to keep old articles? Remember that they can be copied to other folders for storage.*
▶ *The* **Troubleshooting** *options can be turned on if you have problems with your mail or news. The log files could provide useful information for whoever tries to solve the problems.*

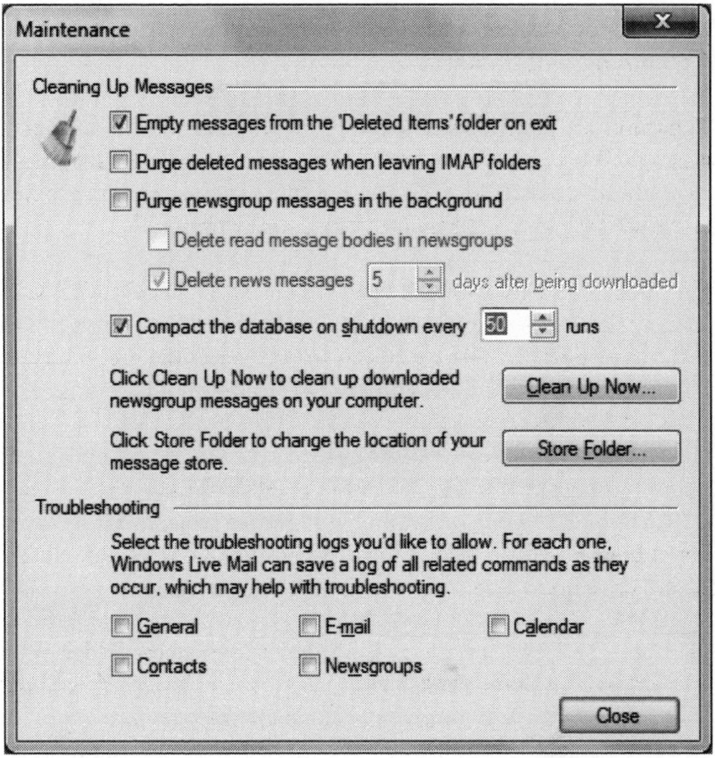

Figure 9.4 Cleaning up messages doesn't just save space – not a problem with big hard disks – it makes it easier to find the stuff you want.

Not sure what to do?

If you are in any doubt about any of the Options, leave them at their default settings – these are fine for most purposes.

LAYOUT OPTIONS

The Message list and Folder pane must always be there, but you have some choices about their display. The Reading pane can be turned off – a message will then be opened in its own window – and you can also turn off the Message Header in the Reading pane. I would be inclined to leave them both on, certainly at first.

1 *Click the Menus button and select Layout...*

2 *Click on the name of an area, e.g. Folder pane, to set its layout options.*

Layout

Reading pane (Mail)
You can use the reading pane to see information about a message or the sender without opening it.
☑ Show the reading pane
  ● At the bottom of the message list
  ○ To the right of the message list

Message list

Folder pane

Message header (Mail)

OK   Cancel   Apply

3 *Click to select from alternative displays or to turn optional elements on or off.*

Keep the Header

With an ordinary message, the Message header isn't really needed – it only tells you what you can find out from the Message list, but if the message has an attached file, it comes in very handy. See Section 9.6 to find out how.

9.5 Live Contacts

You must get e-mail addresses exactly right, or the post won't get through. Unfortunately, addresses are not always user-friendly and are rarely easy to remember. The Contacts is the solution – once you have a correct e-mail address in here you need never worry about it again. When you want to write to someone, you can select the name from the book and start to compose from there, or start the message and then select the names at the **To:** and **Cc:** boxes.

Figure 9.5 My Contacts list – you can store phone numbers and 'snail mail' address details here as well.

ADDING TO THE CONTACTS

If you turn on the option to put people you reply to in your Contacts list (page 190), then you will rarely need to add them by hand – but it is as well to know how.

1 *Open* **Contacts** *from the shortcut in the left-hand pane, or from the* **Go** *menu.*
2 *When the* **Contacts** *window opens, click the* **New** *button or click its arrow and select* **Contact.**

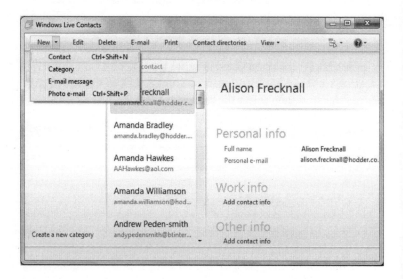

3 *The dialog box has tabs for different sets of contact details, but most of the time you can put in all you need using* **the Quick add** *tab. This should be at the front – select it if it is not.*
4 *Type in the person's first and last names and the e-mail address. These are the only essential details. Add the phone and company details if you like.*

5 *Switch to the* **Contact** *area to add phone numbers or other e-mail addresses.*

Add a Contact

Quick add	First name:	Middle name:
Contact	Joe	
Personal		
Work	Last name:	Nickname:
IM	Green	
Notes		
IDs	Home phone:	Personal e-mail:
	Work phone:	Work e-mail:
	+39 02 88 79 1	JoeGreen@lascala.org.it
	Mobile phone:	Other e-mail:
	Other phone:	Primary e-mail address:
		Personal

[Add contact] [Cancel]

6 *Use the* **Personal** *area to add snail mail addresses and personal details, such as birthday.*

7 *Click* **Add contact.**

Instant addition

If you receive a message from someone who is not in your Contacts, there will be an Add contact link beside their name in the header of the message. Click on it to open the New Contact window – their details will already be in place. Edit them if necessary and click Add contact.

USING THE CONTACTS LIST

When you want to write an address in a new message, click the To: icon to open the **Send an E-mail** panel. This shows the names in your Contacts list. Pick the recipients one at a time, clicking **To->**, **Cc->**, or **Bcc->** to copy them to the appropriate categories. Click **OK** when you've done. The recipients will appear as names, rather than e-mail addresses – don't worry. They will be translated into addresses before sending.

Figure 9.6 Using the Send an E-mail panel to get addresses from your Contacts list. If you add a name by mistake, select it and press [Delete].

Mail from Contacts

If the Contacts list is open already, you can start a new message to someone by selecting their name and clicking on their address. The **New Message** window will open, with the name in the **To:** box.

9.6 Files by mail

Files of any type – graphics, word processor and spreadsheet documents, audio and video clips – and URL links, can be attached to messages and sent by e-mail. Compared to sending files printed or on disk in the post, e-mail is almost always quicker, often more reliable and cheaper.

To attach a file:

1 *Start the new message as normal, adding the recipient's address and typing the Subject line.*
2 *Click the **Attach** button.*
3 *Browse for the file and click **Open**.*
4 *Complete the message and send as usual. There may be a slight delay before the message is sent, as Mail has to convert the file into a special format for sending by mail.*

Figure 9.7 Attaching a file to a message. Any kinds of files can be attached this way, though there are other – easier – ways of attaching pictures (see Section 9.7).

DETACHING FILES

If a message has a file attached to it, there will be a little paperclip icon on the left of its entry in the Message list. Look out for these!

Detaching files from messages used to be hard work – they had to be cut out from the text of the message and processed through special decoding software. With Live Mail, it's a piece of cake.

If the Message header is present it will show the names of any attached files. If it is not there, you will have to use the Save Attachment command on the File menu. Turn on the Message headers and make life easier!

1 *Right-click on the name of the attached file to open the menu.*
2 *Select* **Open** *if you are sure that the file is safe. (See the Warning!)*

Or

3 *Select* **Save As** *and save the file to disk. If there are several files, you can use Save All to save them all at once – they will all go into the same folder.*

Figure 9.8 Attached files can be opened from within the message or saved to disk.

Warning!

Any executable file can contain viruses. Executable include programs (with an .exe extension), screensavers (.scr) batch files (.bat) and – less obviously – documents and spreadsheets, which may contain macros – a set of instructions to the software. Photos and pictures (JPG, PNG, TIF) are safe. Never open an executable file or document sent by an unknown person. Even if the file was sent by a friend, if you have any doubts about it do not open it.

9.7 E-mailing photos

Photos can be sent as attachments, but they can also be inserted into the body of the message, in a special format. The photos are reduced so that they will fit on the page (several levels of reduction are available) and can have text attached to them.

If you have already started the message, use the Add photo button on the toolbar, if not there is a New option you can use. We'll try that.

1 *Click the arrow by the* **New** *button and select* **Photo e-mail.**

2 *Live Mail will open the New Message window and also start the* **Open** *dialog box, in your Picture library or whichever folder you last used.*

3 *Select a photo and click* **Add.**
4 *Add more if required.*
5 *Click* **Done.**

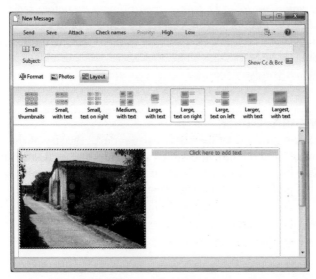

6 *Back at the New Message window, click the* **Layout** *button and select a picture size and layout.*

7 *If you want to add a frame or edit the photo before sending, click the* **Photos** *button to get the editing toolbar.*
8 *Type your text, and don't forget to fill in the* **To:** *address and* **Subject** *lines.*
9 *When you have finished, send it as usual.*

Slow connection?

Reducing the size of the photos also reduces the size of the message and the time it takes to send or receive it. Remember this is if either you or the person you are sending the photos to has a slow Internet connection.

THINGS TO REMEMBER

▶ *Live Mail handles mail through a set of folders. The key ones are the Inbox, where incoming mail is stored, the Outbox, where messages are held if they cannot be sent immediately, and the Sent folder where copies of outgoing messages are stored.*

▶ *The subjects in the header lines should give you an idea of the nature of a message. You can easily reply to, or forward on, incoming mail.*

▶ *When composing a new message, you can use Stationery and apply formatting to the text.*

▶ *Messages can be sent immediately, or stored and sent later when you go online.*

▶ *The Options control your interaction with the system, and how and when messages are sent and read.*

▶ *Use the Contacts list to store the e-mail addresses of your contacts, and you will only have to type an address once!*

▶ *Files can be attached to messages and sent by e-mail. Files attached to incoming messages can be opened or saved.*

▶ *For sending photos, you can use the Photo e-mail format.*

SELF TEST

1 If Live Mail is not already on your computer, where can you get it from?

2 Why should you bother with the Subject line?

3 What are the Cc and Bcc boxes used for?

4 Someone new has just written to you. How can you quickly add their address to your Contacts?

5 How do you add an address from the Contacts list to a message?

6 Is a message lost forever if you delete it?

7 If you want to include the text of messages when you reply to them, what do you need to do?

8 What is the difference between sending a photo as an attachment, or as an insert in a message?

10

....

Control Panel

10.1 Using the Panel

Windows' plug and play facility for new hardware, and the
installation routines for new software, help to ensure that your
system is properly configured. However, there are some things
which Windows cannot do for you as they depend upon your
preferences. The Control Panel is where you find the tools to
customize your setup to suit yourself. In this chapter we will be
looking at eight of the key components. Even if you are happy
with the way that your system is running – or if you are hesitant
about making changes that you might regret – do have a look at
these. All the dialog boxes have a **Cancel** button!

▶ *To open the Control Panel, click the* **Start** *button then click
the* **Control Panel** *link on the right-hand side.*

The panel has three alternative displays. Switch between them by
selecting from the options on the **View by** list:

▶ **Category** *view is probably the best view for new users.
It groups the components by function and guides you through
the tasks.*
▶ *The* **Large** *and* **Small icon** *views are similar to the displays in
earlier versions of Windows. They show all the components,
and for the most part – though not always – it is obvious
which you should use to customize which part of your PC.*

We'll work through the default Category view.

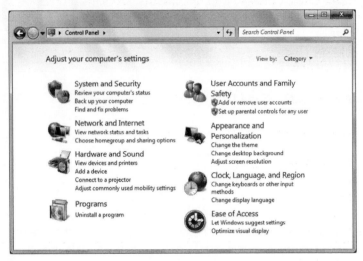

Figure 10.1 The Control Panel in category view.

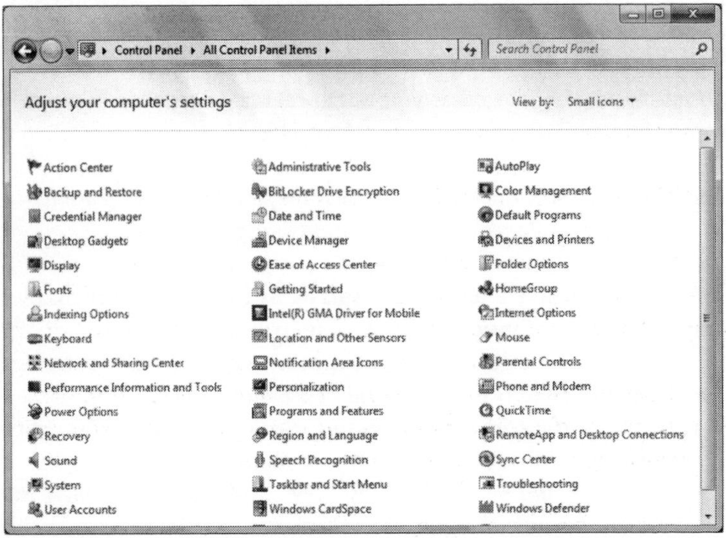

Figure 10.2 The Control Panel in small icons view. Even if you are new to Windows, you may find it worthwhile switching to this as it does give you a direct route to the components – and it is usually pretty obvious what each component does.

10.2 Programs

Any software that is written to the Windows specifications will be registered with the system when it is installed, so that it can be uninstalled, or the installation adjusted later through this facility.

UNINSTALL OR CHANGE A PROGRAM

Use this to clear unwanted software off your system, or to add or remove components from suites, such as Microsoft Office. If you simply delete a program's folder in Explorer, it may remove all or most of the software's files – though there may be others scattered elsewhere in your disks – but it will not remove the entry in the Start menu, or the File Types associations. A proper uninstall will (normally) do a full clean-out from your system.

1 *In the* **Programs** *category, click* **Uninstall a program.**
2 *At the* **Uninstall or change programs** *window, select the program.*

3 *Click the* **Uninstall** *button in the toolbar. (Notice that some programs have a Repair option – this can be useful if software becomes corrupted or components accidentally deleted.)*

4 *The uninstall routines vary between programs, but you will normally be asked to confirm before the program is uninstalled.*

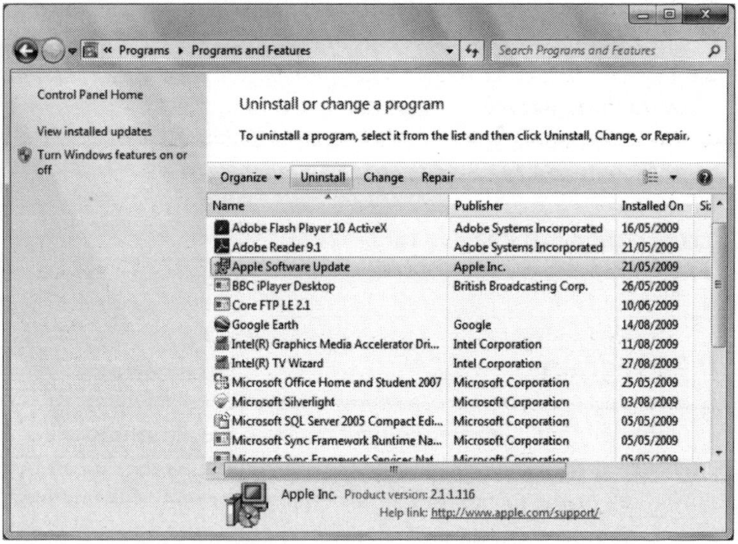

Figure 10.3 Starting to uninstall a program.

WINDOWS FEATURES

Windows 7 is a huge package with a vast set of utilities and accessories – most people will use only a limited number of these and no one will use all of them. You may decide, after having used Windows for a while, that some components are a waste of space – and then again, you may need to put them back later!

1 *In the* **Uninstall or change programs** *window, click the* **Turn Windows features on and off** *link in the Tasks list on the left.*

The components are listed, with a checkbox beside the name
to indicate its status, and a disk space given on the right.
The checkboxes can be in one of three states:

- ▶ *a tick shows all components are selected under this heading*
- ▶ *a blue block shows that some components are selected*
- ▶ *an empty box shows that no components are selected.*

2 *A Plus icon beside a heading shows that it has subcomponents –
click on the icon to display them.*
3 *Tick the checkbox to add a component, or clear it to remove
an existing one.*
4 *Click* **OK** *when you have finished and wait while Windows
adds or removes components. You may have to restart the PC
for some changes to take effect.*

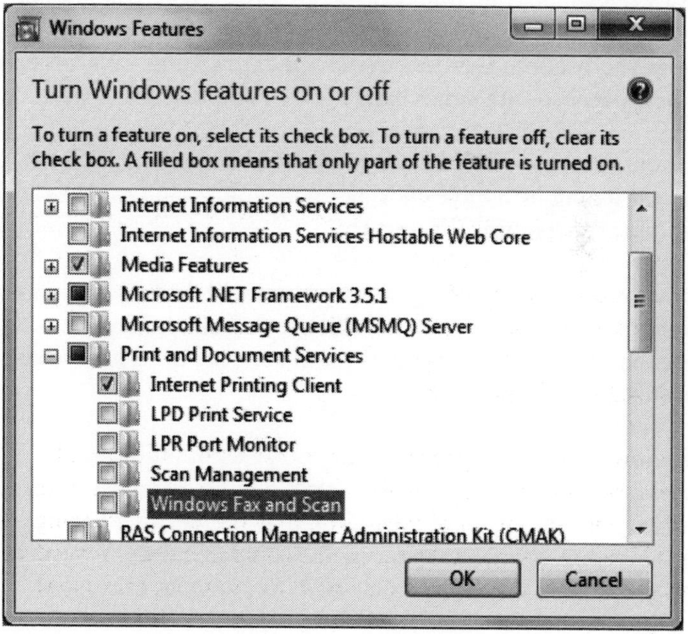

Figure 10.4 Adjusting the Windows features. If you are not sure what a feature does – and some are quite
technical! – don't change its setting.

10.3 Mouse

We configured the mouse pointers back in Chapter 6. That was just decorative – other aspects of the mouse are more important.

▶ *Go to the* **Hardware and Sound** *area and click the* **Mouse** *link.*

BUTTONS

The first tab of the **Mouse Properties** panel is for the **Buttons**.

If you are left-handed, you may be tempted by the **Switch primary and secondary buttons** option (so you would use the one on the right for a simple click, and left-click to open context menus). Resist the temptation. It may make life easier when you first start to use your new PC, but you will be in a mess if you ever have to use anybody else's. Get used to the standard setting – it's not hard, I use my mouse with either hand.

The only crucial setting here is the **Double-click speed**. Test the current setting by double-clicking on the folder, and use the slider to adjust the response if necessary.

If you have trouble holding down a button while dragging, you might like to try turning on the **ClickLock** facility. Tick the checkbox then click the Settings button and set the time to wait before turning a 'click' into a 'lock'.

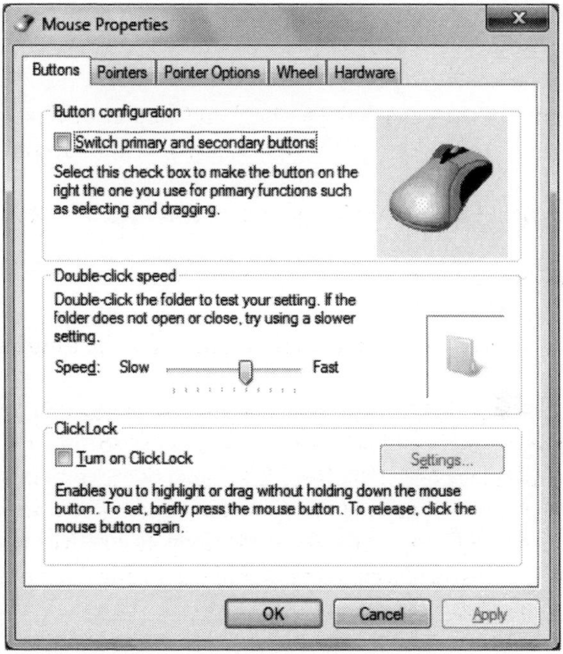

Figure 10.5 *When the double-click speed is right for you, you should be able to open and close the test icon easily.*

POINTER OPTIONS

The **Motion** area controls how far and how fast the pointer moves in relation to the mouse movement. To test this, move the mouse and watch the pointer. If you don't feel comfortably in control of it, drag the slider towards **Slow**. If it's taking too long to get around, set it faster. Click **OK** when it feels right.

Under **Visibility**, you might want to turn on **Pointer trails** if you are working on a laptop PC. Pointers do not show up well on some LCD screens, particularly when they are in motion. Turning on the trail makes them much easier to see. Likewise, turning on **Show location of pointer** can be handy if you have trouble finding it. With it on, when you press [**Control**] a circle will appear around the pointer and shrink onto it.

On the **Wheel** tab you can set the scrolling speed of the wheel.

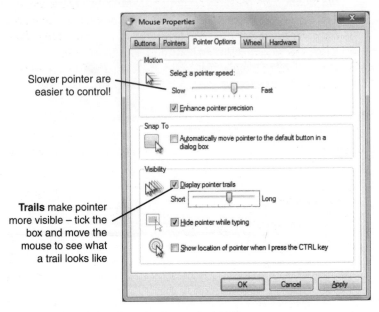

Slower pointer are easier to control!

Trails make pointer more visible – tick the box and move the mouse to see what a trail looks like

Figure 10.6 The Pointer Options tab controls pointer speed and visibility.

10.4 Clock, Language and Region

CHANGE THE DATE AND TIME

Even if you do not display the Clock in the Notification Area of the Taskbar (see page 235), you should still make sure that the clock/calendar is correctly set if you want the date and time details to be right on your saved documents. PCs are good time-keepers – Windows even adjusts for Summer Time automatically – as long as they are set correctly at the start.

1 *Go to the* **Clock, Language and Region** *area and select* **Date and time.**
2 *At the* **Date and Time** *dialog box, click the* **Change date and time** *button.*

3 To change the date, click on the month/year heading then pick the month from the full year display. Set the day by clicking on it.
4 To change the time, select the hour or minute figure and type the correct value, or use the little arrows to adjust the values.
5 Click **OK** to return to the **Date and Time** dialog box.
6 If you need to change the time zone, click the **Change time zone** button and select the zone from the drop-down list.

If you use the PC to connect to the Internet, you can keep your clock accurate by turning on the synchronization option on the **Internet Time** tab. The PC will then synchronize regularly with an Internet time server.

Figure 10.7 Setting the time – if necessary, click Change time zone and pick one from the list. Click Change date and time to set the clock or the calendar.

Figure 10.8 Setting the date – click on the month name if you need to change the month.

You can also get to the Date and Time dialog box by right-clicking on the clock in the Taskbar and selecting Adjust date/time in the shortcut menu.

DATE, TIME AND NUMBER FORMATS

In the Clock, Language and Region area, under **Regional and Language Options** you will find **Change the date, time or number format.** On the **Formats** tab you will see samples of the formats currently used for numbers, currency, time and dates. If you are happy to use the formats that are standard for your region, then all you need to do is select the country from the **Current format** drop-down list.

If you want to vary any of the settings, click the bar to drop down its menu and choose and alternative formats.

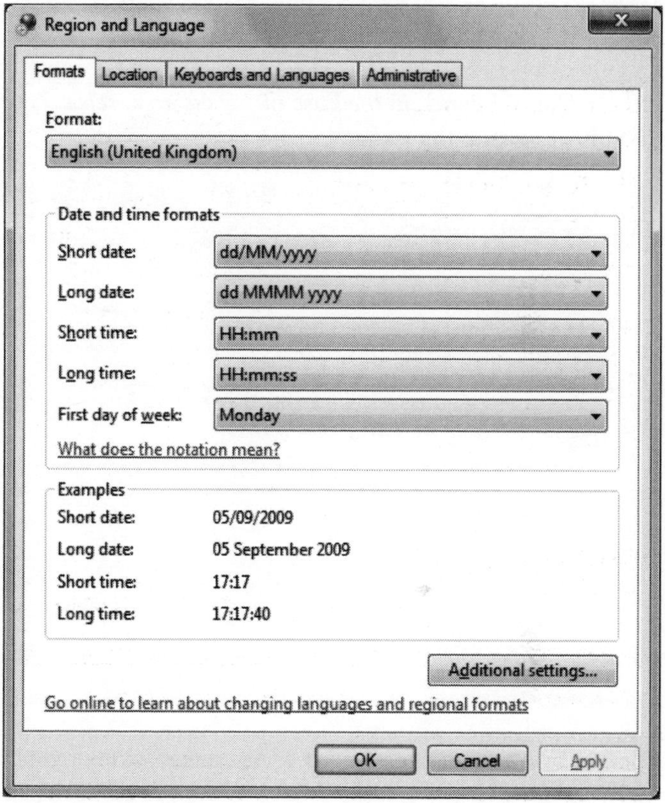

Figure 10.9 Setting the Regional Options.

10.5 Ease of Access

The options here are designed to make life easier for people with disabilities, with the main emphasis on visual disabilities, but there are also other tools that can make life easier for anyone who is less than comfortable with the keyboard or mouse.

GET RECOMMENDATIONS

Probably the best way to approach this is to see what Windows has to offer.

1 *At the* **Control Panel,** *in the* **Ease of Access** *area, select* **Let Windows suggest the settings.**

2 *You will be taken through a set of five panels, asking about your (or the user's if you are setting this up for someone else) eyesight, dexterity, hearing, speech and reasoning.*
3 *Windows will list those facilities which may help with access. Tick the checkbox for those which you would like to try.*

Recommended settings

These settings can help you set up your computer to meet your needs. Review the recommended settings below and select the options that you want to use.

☐ Turn on Narrator

Narrator reads aloud any text on the screen. You will need speakers.

☑ Turn on Magnifier

Magnifier zooms in anywhere on the screen, and makes everything in that area larger. You can move Magnifier around, lock it in one place, or resize it.

☑ Make the focus rectangle thicker

Set the thickness of the blinking cursor: `1 ▼`   Preview: `│`

☐ Turn on Sticky Keys

Press keyboard shortcuts (such as CTRL+ALT+DEL) one key at a time.

Set up Sticky Keys

☐ Turn on Toggle Keys

Hear a tone when you press CAPS LOCK, NUM LOCK, or SCROLL LOCK.

☑ Turn on Toggle Keys by holding down the NUM LOCK key for 5 seconds

[OK] [Cancel] [Apply]

You can change the settings

You can turn the accessibility features off again if you decide that they are no help, or go back through the routine and turn others on. And you can do this whenever you like – though note that you have to restart the computer before some changes take effect.

NARRATOR

This reads the text off the screen, the labels on buttons and the descriptions of images (if present). You can change the volume, pitch and speed of the voice – all of which help to make it much easier to listen to – but not the accent. Though intended for people with severe sight problems, it can be used in other situations where you want to be able to listen to text, perhaps while doing something else.

MAGNIFIER

This displays the active area at anything from twice to 16 times the normal size – and the active area can be any or all of the mouse position, the current typing location, or wherever any other keys have placed the focus. The Magnifier can fill the whole screen, or be run in a strip across the top, or in a rectangular lens. Its Taskbar button opens a small control window where you can select the View mode, set the magnification and open an Options dialog box. The options are limited – but crucially you can adjust the width and depth of the lens from here.

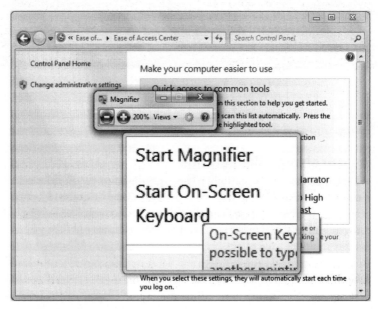

Figure 10.10 The Magnifier in use.

HIGH CONTRAST

You can set up the high contrast, large font display so that it can be turned on and off as needed by the key combination [**Shift**] + [**Alt**] + [**Print Screen**].

Figure 10.11 The high contrast display can make text easier to read, but can make icon-based work more difficult. Being able to toggle between this and normal is better than setting the screen always to high contrast.

ON-SCREEN KEYBOARD

If typing at a keyboard is a problem for any reason, this may be a viable alternative. The on-screen keyboard can be operated by a mouse or other pointing device. As you can only click on one key at a time, the [Shift], [Ctrl] and [Alt] keys are set to remain selected until a second key has been clicked.

By default it sits on top of all other windows, but you can set it to drop beneath the active window. Options on the Keyboard and Settings menus allow you to adjust the layout and how it is used.

Figure 10.12 The On-Screen Keyboard.

MAKE THE KEYBOARD EASIER TO USE

Windows may recommend some or all of these to make the keyboard easier to use.

▶ **Sticky Keys** *allow you to get the [Shift], [Ctrl] and [Alt] key combinations by pressing them in sequence rather than simultaneously.*

▶ **Toggle Keys** *will alert you when the Caps Lock, Num Lock or Scroll Lock keys are pressed. This is handy if, like me, you sometimes hit Caps Lock when aiming for Tab, and then type merrily on in CAPITALS!*

▶ **Filter Keys** *control the point at which a keystroke is picked up, or is repeated, and the repeat rate. Most of these settings can also be controlled through the Keyboard component. If you still find that the keys are not responding as you would like after you have set the options there, come back and check out Filter Keys.*

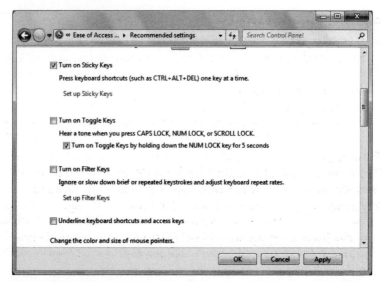

Figure 10.13 Some keyboard options in the ease of access center.

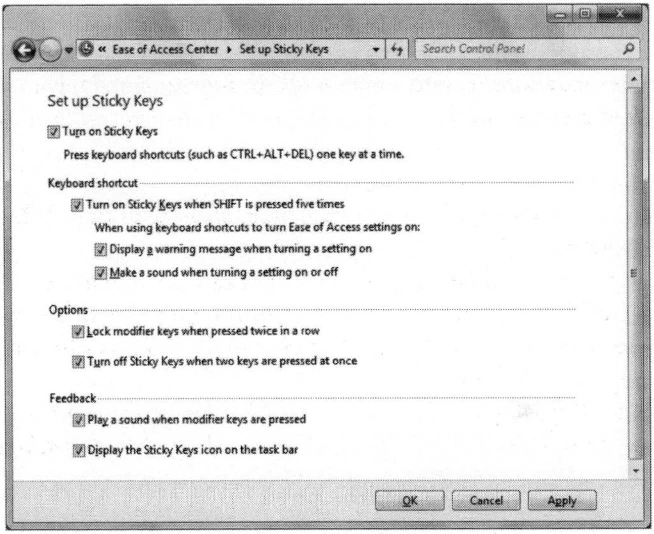

Figure 10.14 Configuring the Sticky Keys options to your needs. Most of the ease of access features have similar settings panels, and notice the keyboard shortcut option. If used, the feature can be turned on and off – either to suit different users, or to suit the way you are working at that time.

Prefer keys to the mouse?

If you find the mouse hard to handle, you can turn on **Mouse Keys**, which you use number pad keys to make mouse actions:

[5] does the left-click;
[-] and [5] do the right-click;
the remaining number keys move the mouse.

Filter keys

These options can filter out unintentional keystrokes, and there are basically two ways in which these can be produced: by hitting a key accidentally, or by keeping a key held down too long.

▶ *The* **Bounce** **key** *option will tell the keyboard to ignore brief keystrokes – you can set the minimum time for holding a key down before it is accepted.*

▶ The **Repeat keys and Slow keys** *options let you set the minimum times for holding down keys before they start to repeat. You normally want keystrokes to be picked up separately, but will sometimes want them to repeat – perhaps to create a line of * * * * * *. You can also filter out brief strokes from here.*

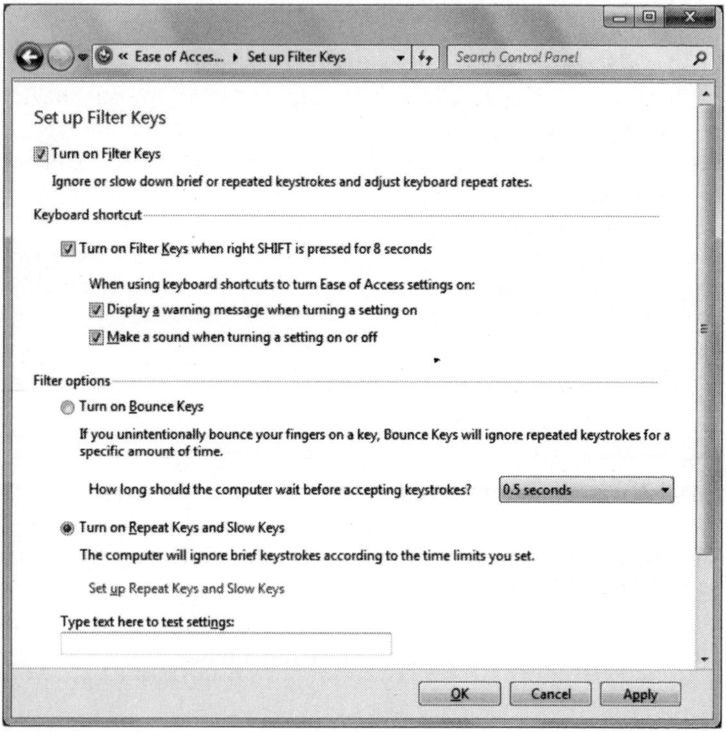

Figure 10.15 Setting up Filter Keys. You can turn on either the bounce keys or repeat keys options, though the repeat options also include a 'bounce' filter.

10.6 User Accounts

Windows makes it easy for several people to share the use of one PC. Each user can have their own set of folders and their own customized Desktop and Start menu.

You can only create accounts if you have an Administrator level account, or if yours is the only account.

1 *In the* User Accounts and Family Safety *area in the Control Panel, click* Add or remove a user account.
2 *Click* Create a new account.
3 *Enter the user's name and click* Next.
4 *Set the account type. This should be* Standard *unless the user needs to be able to add software, or add users or make other changes to the system.*
5 *Click* Create Account. *The new user can later set or change their password or change their picture.*

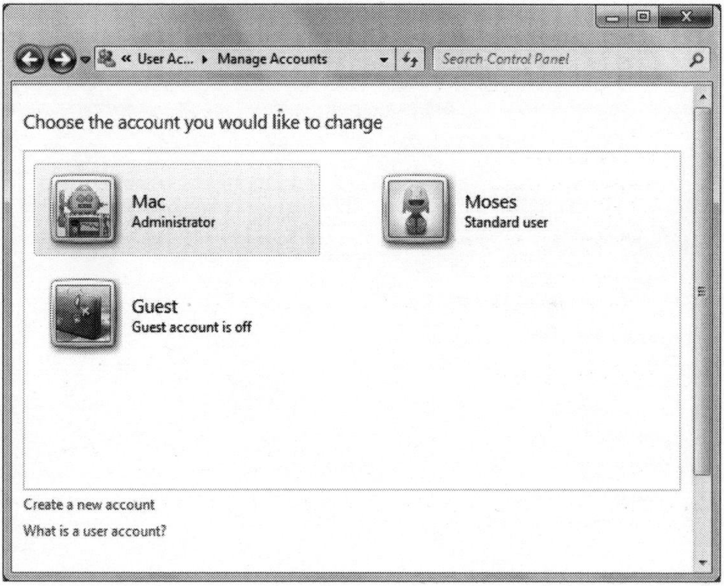

Figure 10.16 The User Accounts panel.

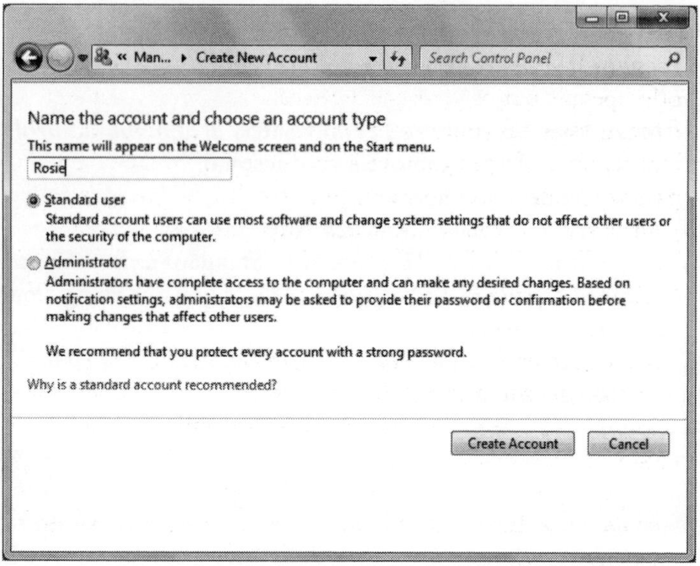

Figure 10.17 Users should normally be set as standard.

Figure 10.18 The User Accounts panel for a standard user.

Passwords

Passwords should only be created if needed, e.g. to keep other people out of your private area, or to prevent others from messing up your system, either from ignorance or malice. If you forget your password, use the link to create a password reset disk. If you do not do this, and then forget your password, you will lose access to your own data!

PARENTAL CONTROLS

Windows gives parents the ability to control how and when children use the computer. You can set controls on the times they can use the computer, what games they can play and which programs they can use.

1 *In the* **User Accounts and Family Safety** *area, click* **Set up parental controls**.
2 *Click on the child's account.*
3 *Turn on parental controls.*
4 *Go to each* **Windows Settings** *section in turn. Choose the level of restrictions that you think is appropriate and click* **OK**.
5 *Back at the main set-up window, click* **OK** *to apply the new settings.*

The settings can be adjusted at any time to reflect the child's growing maturity.

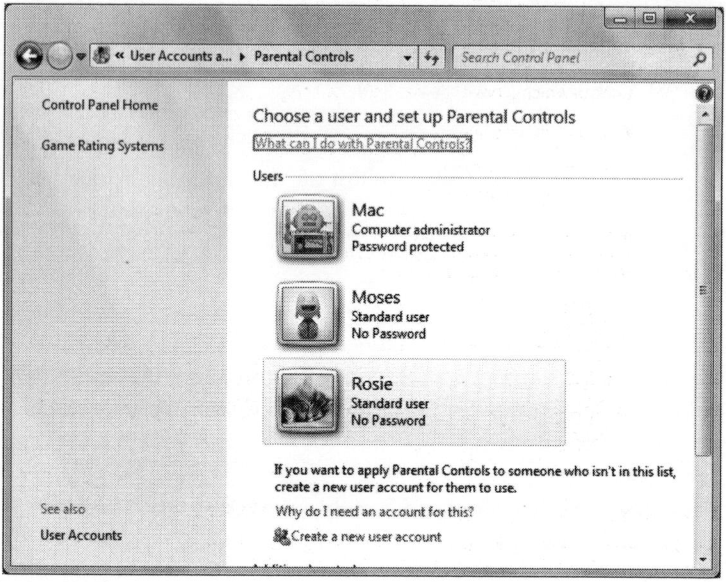

Figure 10.19 Starting to set up controls for a child user.

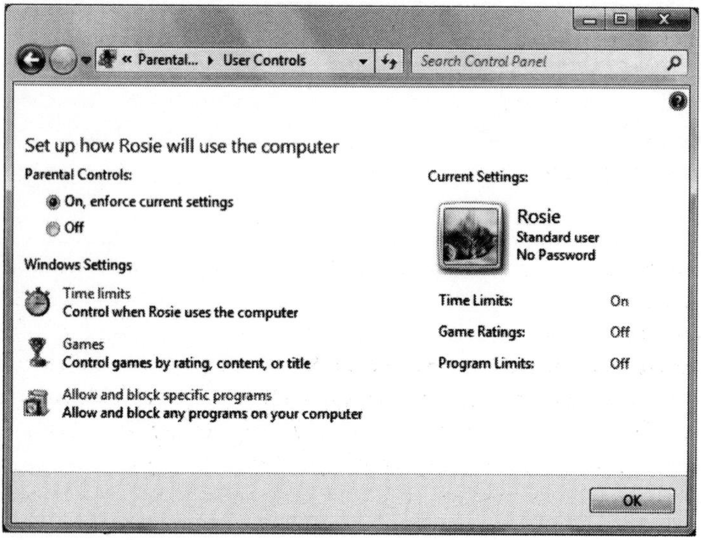

Figure 10.20 Set the restrictions to suit your child.

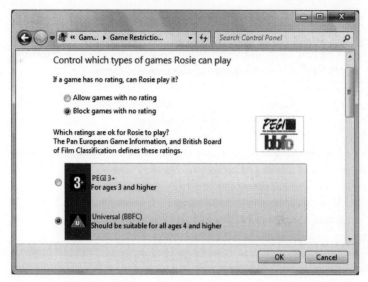

Figure 10.21 If you have games on the PC for older children or adults, or if they can be accessed through the Internet, you may want to keep the younger ones away from them.

Further safeguards

You can set limits to children's access to websites through Internet Explorer.

THINGS TO REMEMBER

▶ You can configure your system to suit your way of working through the components of the Control Panel.

▶ Use Programs and Features to add or remove the components of application suites and of Windows.

▶ Use the Mouse panel to set the double-click response and the speed at which the mouse moves the pointer.

▶ You can change the date or time, through the Date/Time panel.

▶ The Ease of Access options can make the mouse and keyboard easier to use, and the screen easier to see.

▶ If several people use the PC, you can set up and configure separate, secure user accounts for them.

▶ Parental Controls can be set on accounts if wanted.

SELF TEST

1 *What different view modes are available in the Control Panel and how can you select them?*

2 *How can you clear unwanted programs off your system?*

3 *In what ways can you customize the mouse?*

4 *If you need to change the time zone, where would you start?*

5 *Which ease of access feature can help someone who has difficulty seeing the details on a screen?*

6 *What is the difference between a Standard and an Administrator user account?*

7 *How can you restrict a child's activity on the computer?*

Taskbar and Start menu

11.1 Taskbar options

By now you should be familiar with using the Taskbar and Start
menu in your Windows sessions. Here we will look at ways in
which you can customize the Taskbar and reorganize the Start
menu. The techniques are simple and worth learning – these are
two elements of the Windows system that you use regularly, so you
should have them set up to your way of working. The Properties
panel for the Taskbar and Start Menu can be opened by right-
clicking on the Taskbar or the Start button and selecting **Properties.**

Toolbars	▶
Cascade windows	
Show windows stacked	
Show windows side by side	
Show the desktop	
Start Task Manager	
✓ Lock the taskbar	
Properties	

On the **Taskbar** tab you will see six on/off options which affect its
appearance and working in various ways.

- ▶ **Lock the taskbar** – *fixes the current position of the Taskbar and of its toolbars. Unlock it if you want to adjust the layout.*
- ▶ **Auto hide** – *if set, the Taskbar slides off-screen when not in use. Pointing off the screen makes it pop-up again. With a small screen, turn this on to maximize the working area.*
- ▶ **Use small icons** – *this may be useful if you tend to run a lot of programs at once.*
- ▶ *The* **Taskbar location** *can be on any of the four sides of the screen. I've never actually met anyone who has it anywhere other than across the bottom, but you may want to be different.*
- ▶ *The* **Taskbar buttons** *can be presented in three ways – see below.*
- ▶ **Aero Peek** *can be turned off if not wanted.*

Figure 11.1 Setting the Taskbar options.

What's Aero Peek?

Over on the far right of the Taskbar is the Show Desktop button. Click this and all open windows are minimized down to Taskbar buttons. When Aero Peek is on, if you point to the Show Desktop button, the open windows become transparent so that you can see the Desktop.

TASKBAR BUTTONS

The buttons can be displayed in three ways:

Never Combine – shows the Title bar information (i.e. the name of the document or folder) beside the icon and keeps each button separate on the Taskbar. Once there are more than five or six buttons on the Taskbar, they will get squeezed up, so that less of the writing is visible.

Combine when Taskbar is full – if you have several windows of the same program, e.g. three Word documents, they will be represented by a single button when the Taskbar gets crowded. If you point at the button, thumbnails of the windows will appear above it, and clicking on one of these will switch you to that window.

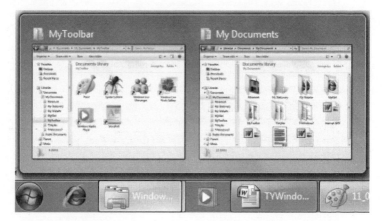

Always combine, hide labels – gives the most compact display.

NOTIFICATION AREA

The Notification area holds icons for system programs and for utilities, such as anti-virus software, that work in the background when the PC is running. When one of these utilities does something, or finds a problem, it puts up a message to notify you – hence the name.

If you click the Customize button in the **Notification area** part of the Taskbar properties panel, you can control which icons to display and which notification to see. For each utility, you can show or hide the icon and notifications, or just show the notifications.

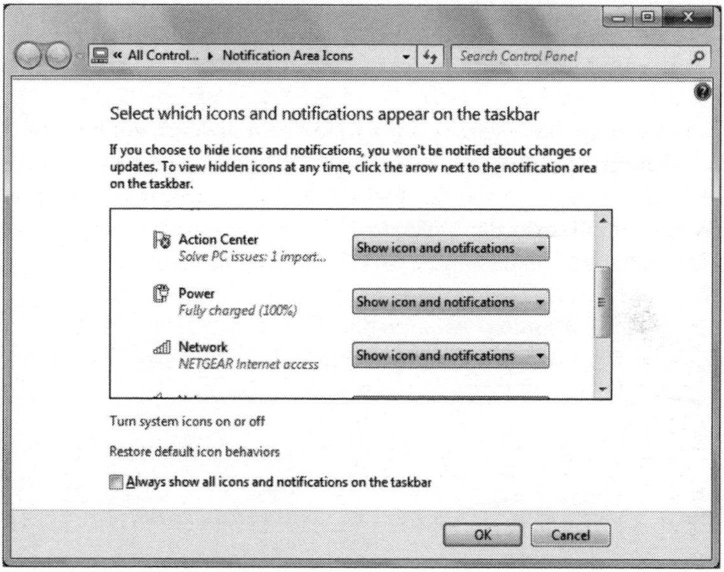

Figure 11.2 Setting the Notification Area options.

11.2 Toolbars

A toolbar can put a utility or a collection of links onto the Taskbar for easy access. There may not be any on your Taskbar yet, but they can be added. There are five ready-made toolbars.

Address – *enter an Internet address here, and Internet Explorer will start and try to connect to it.*

Links – *carries a set of buttons with Internet addresses, clicking one starts Internet Explorer to make the connection.*

Tablet PC Input Panel – *for users with a Tablet PC.*

Desktop – *contains copies of the icons present on the Desktop.*

Language Bar – *for switching the keyboard settings between different languages.*

To add a toolbar to the Taskbar:
1 *Right-click on an empty part of the Taskbar.*
2 *Point to* **Toolbars** *to open the menu.*
3 *Click on a toolbar name to add it.*
4 *And if you decide you don't really want it, go back over the same steps, and click again to remove the tick.*

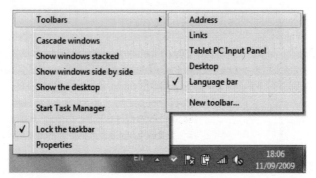

Figure 11.3 Adding toolbars to the Taskbar. Right-click on a blank area of the Taskbar to open the short menu.

CREATING NEW TOOLBARS

If you like working from the Taskbar, you can set up one or more toolbars containing shortcuts to your favourite applications, folders – or Internet links (see Chapter 8):

1 *Create a folder, within* Documents, *and name it* 'MyTools' *or something similar.*
2 *To set up a shortcut to an applications, drag its link directly from the Start menu.*
3 *To set up a link to a folder, run Computer again, and navigate through so that you can see the folder you want to use. Hold the right button down and drag the folder's icon in your toolbar folder, and select* **the Create Shortcut Here** *option.*
4 *If you are going to show text labels on the toolbar, edit the names so that they are as brief as possible or you will have trouble displaying them all.*
5 *When you have assembled your shortcuts, right-click on the Taskbar, point to* **Toolbars** *and select* **New Toolbar...**
6 *Work through the folder display to find the one containing your shortcuts, then click* **Select Folder.**
7 *Click* **OK.**

Figure 11.4 Creating a shortcut for the new toolbar from a Start menu item.

Figure 11.5 The new toolbar folder, almost ready to be added to the Taskbar.

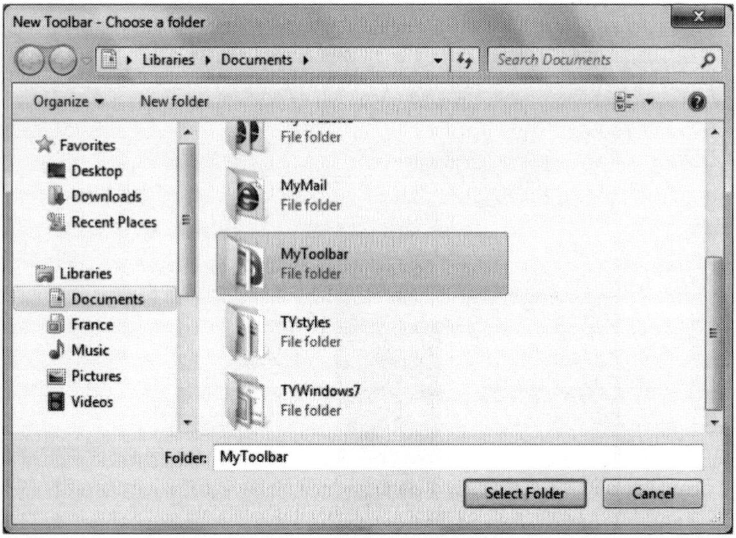

Figure 11.6 Adding the new toolbar.

11.3 The Start menu

Right-click on the **Start** button and select **Properties** from the short menu, to go to the **Start Menu** tab of the **Taskbar and Start Menu Properties** panel. Here you can customize the appearance of the menu, and control which items appear on your menu system, and where.

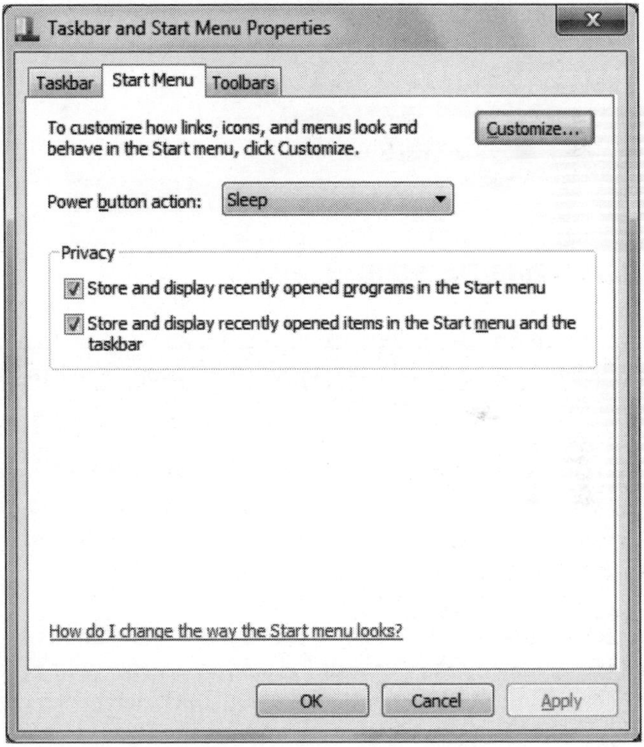

Figure 11.7 The Start menu properties panel.

Notice the **Privacy** options. The list of recently opened files and programs makes it simpler to get back to the last jobs you were doing, but it also makes it easier for other people to see what you have been doing. In an office environment, there could be good reasons why you might want to turn off one or both of the **Store and display** options.

The Power button action allows you to assign any of the shut down/log off/restart/sleep actions to the button. Pick whichever you use most, so you can end a session in two clicks.

Power button action:	Sleep ▼
	Switch user
Privacy	Log off
	Lock
☑ Store and display ...	Restart
	Sleep
☑ Store and display ...	Hibernate
taskbar	Shut down

CUSTOMIZING THE START MENU

Most of the items on the Start menu are optional. If you do not use them, they do not have to be displayed. With many, you can then choose how they are displayed:

▶ *As a link – when you click the item, a folder will open, and you may then pick an item or a subfolder within that folder.*
▶ *As a menu – when you point to the item, a menu appears, listing the subfolders and files within its folder.*

Some items work better as menus, e.g. Games – it is simpler to pick a game from a menu than to wait for a folder to open and pick from there. Some work better as links, e.g. Documents – you would normally want the folder open to work on your files.

1 *Right-click on the* **Start** *button and select* **Properties**.
2 *At the Start menu tab, click the* **Customize** *button.*
3 *Work through the options, thinking about each as you go.*

4 *Where there is a checkbox, a tick turns it on. Note that some of these are optional items, but others control the way the menu behaves.*

5 *Set the* **number of recent programs** *and* **recent items** *to display – these links are convenient, but too many can be confusing.*

6 *Click* **OK** *when you have done.*

7 *Back at the* **Properties** *dialog box, click* **Apply**.

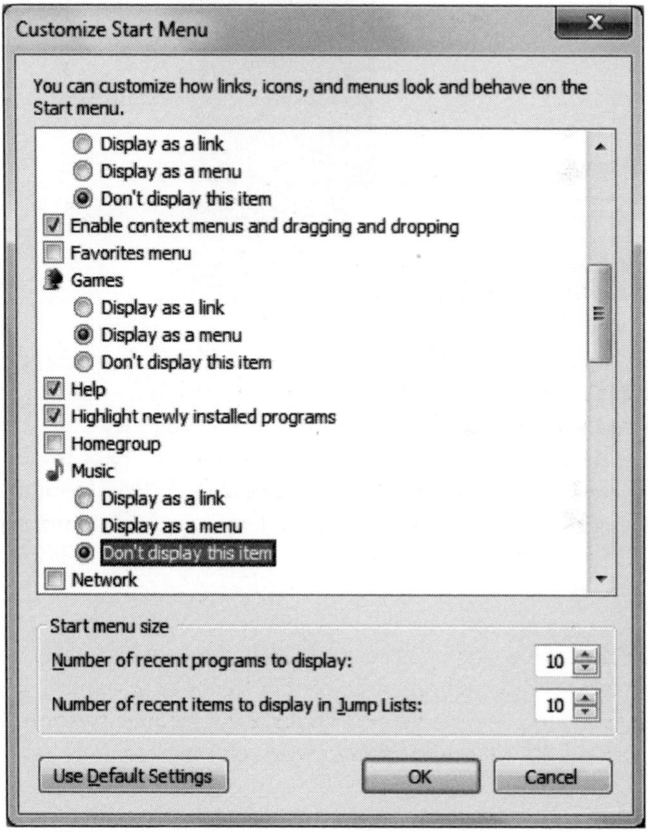

Customize Start Menu

You can customize how links, icons, and menus look and behave on the Start menu.

- ○ Display as a link
- ○ Display as a menu
- ◉ Don't display this item
- ☑ Enable context menus and dragging and dropping
- ☐ Favorites menu
- 🎮 Games
  - ○ Display as a link
  - ◉ Display as a menu
  - ○ Don't display this item
- ☑ Help
- ☑ Highlight newly installed programs
- ☐ Homegroup
- 🎵 Music
  - ○ Display as a link
  - ○ Display as a menu
  - ◉ Don't display this item
- ☐ Network

Start menu size

Number of recent programs to display: 10

Number of recent items to display in Jump Lists: 10

Use Default Settings   OK   Cancel

Figure 11.8 Customizing the Start menu.

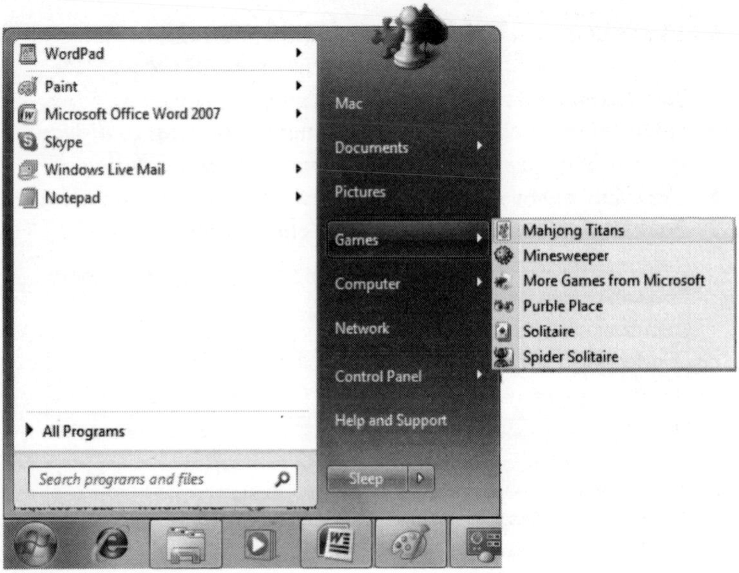

Figure 11.9 A customized Start menu.

No! What have I done?

If you get carried away with your customizing, then find that the new Start menu is not to your liking, go back to Customize Start Menu dialog box and click the Use Default Settings button down in the bottom left to get back to normal.

THINGS TO REMEMBER

▶ *The Taskbar can be displayed on top of all other windows, behind them, or tucked off screen when not in use.*

▶ *Taskbar buttons can be shown with or without text labels, and where there are multiple windows of one program, the buttons can be combined to save space.*

▶ *You can control which icons are displayed in the Notification Area.*

▶ *Ready-made toolbars can be added to the Taskbar.*

▶ *You can create your own folders of shortcuts and turn them into Taskbar toolbars.*

▶ *You can customize the appearance and the selection of shortcuts on the Start menu.*

SELF TEST

1 *If you want to change anything about the Taskbar or Start menu, where do you start?*

2 *The Taskbar is so useful, why would anyone want to hide it?*

3 *What is the Notification Area?*

4 *What is the point of adding toolbars to the Taskbar?*

5 *In what ways can you change the appearance and content of the Start menu through the Properties dialog box?*

12

Accessories

12.1 WordPad

Don't underrate WordPad just because it's free. It has all the
facilities that you would have found in the top-flight software a
few years ago, and compares well with today's commercial
packages. It's fine for writing letters, essays, reports, source
code for computer programs and anything else where you want
to be able to edit text efficiently, format it with different fonts,
styles and colours, and perhaps incorporate graphics or other
files.

▶ *When entering text, just keep typing when you reach
  the edge of the page – the text will be wrapped round to
  the next line. Only press the* **Enter** *key at the end of a
  paragraph.*
▶ *Existing text can be selected, with the normal techniques
  (see section 4.1), then moved, deleted or formatted.*
▶ *Most formatting can be done through the Ribbon. Select the
  text, then pick a font or size from the drop-down lists, or click
  the bold, italic, underline, colour or other buttons in the Font
  group.*
▶ *The left, centre and right alignment buttons determine how the
  text lines up with the edges of the paper.*
▶ *The bullets button indents text from the left, with a blob at the
  start of each paragraph.*

▶ *Alignment and bullet formats apply to whole paragraphs. You do not need to select the whole paragraph – if the cursor is within it, or part of its text is selected, the paragraph will be formatted.*

WordPad button   Ruler   Ribbon

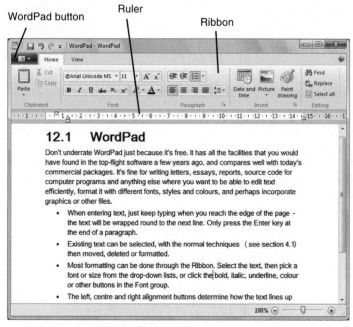

Figure 12.1 WordPad, being used to create the text for these pages. If there is an arrow beside a button, clicking the arrow will open a list or palette of options. Clicking the button itself will apply the current setting.

THE RIBBON AND THE MENU

The Ribbon holds all the tools and commands that you need for creating and editing your documents. They are arranged in groups of related tools, on two tabs.

The Home tab holds those that you will need most often – for editing and formatting your text and for inserting pictures and other objects.

On the View tab you can zoom in and out, turn the Ruler and Status bar on or off, and set the word wrap mode and units of measurement.

Click on a tab's name to bring it to the front.

Figure 12.2 The ribbon in WordPad with the view tab at the front.

The commands for opening, closing, saving, printing and otherwise doing things with the whole document are on a menu which drops down from the WordPad button. You will find this to the left of the tab names, above the Ribbon. The commands are listed down the left. On the right are the names of recently used files. If you point to a command which has options, e.g. Save As gives you a choice of formats, these will be displayed on the right.

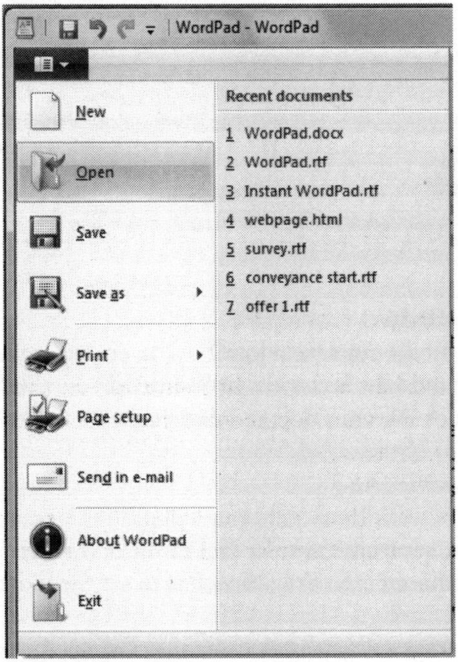

WordPad - WordPad

New

Open

Save

Save as ▶

Print ▶

Page setup

Send in e-mail

About WordPad

Exit

Recent documents

1 WordPad.docx
2 WordPad.rtf
3 Instant WordPad.rtf
4 webpage.html
5 survey.rtf
6 conveyance start.rtf
7 offer 1.rtf

Figure 12.3 The menu in WordPad.

The Quick Access Toolbar

On the left of the Title bar is the Quick Access Toolbar which can hold icons to give you one-click access to the menu commands. This will be almost empty at first, but you can easily add more icons – just click the arrows at the end and tick the ones you want to show. New, Open and Quick Print are well worth adding.

Figure 12.4 The Quick Access Toolbar. Click the arrow to open the Customize menu where you can add or remove icons, and set the Ribbon display options.

Undo and Redo

Undo and Redo can save a lot of work, correcting mistakes, mistyping and bad decisions. In WordPad you will find them on the Quick Access Toolbar – and only there.

INDENTS AND TABS

These are best set from the ruler. Select the text where new indents or tabs are required then drag the icons to set the indent; click to set a tab point.

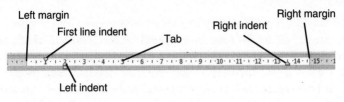

Figure 12.5 The ruler.

GRAPHICS AND OTHER OBJECTS

Pictures, graphs, spreadsheets, audio and video clips – in fact just about any object that can be produced by any Windows application – can be incorporated into a WordPad document. You can't do fancy layouts with WordPad. An object can sit by itself, separate from the text above and below, or can be embedded in a single line, and that's it.

Pictures are especially easy to insert.

1   *Click the* **Picture** *button in the* **Insert** *group on the Ribbon.*
2   *Browse through your folders to find the file.*
3   *Select the file and click* **Open.**

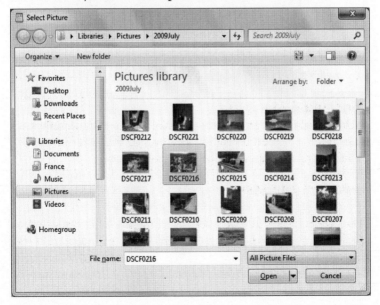

4 Back in WordPad, you can move or resize the object. Select it – it will be outlined with handles at the corners and edges. Point to a handle to get the double-headed arrow then drag in or out as required. The position of the object across the page can be set by using the alignment buttons.

Figure 12.6 Adjusting the size of an image in WordPad.

Other types of object

A little more work is required to insert other types of object. Start by clicking the dialog box launcher – the little arrow at the bottom right of the Insert group.

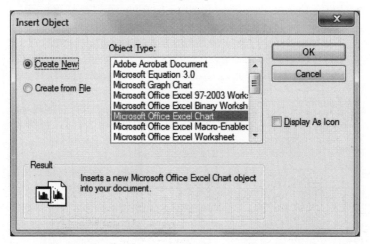

▶ *If the object does not exist, pick* **Create New***, select the* **Object Type** *and click* **OK***. The appropriate application will open. When you have created the object, save it if you want to keep a separate copy for future use, then select the* **Exit & Return to Document** *option from the* **File** *menu.*
▶ *If you want to use an existing object, select* **Create from File***, and browse through your folders to locate it.*

An inserted object can be edited by double-clicking on it – this opens the source application. Use **Exit & Return** when you have finished editing.

PAGE SETUP

The **Page Setup** panel, opened from the **WordPad** menu, controls the basic size and layout of the page – for all pages in the document.

- *The* **Paper Size** *and* **Source** *settings rarely need changing – if you've set your printer properties correctly. If you are printing on card or special paper, change the* **Source** *to* **Manual,** *if the option is available.*
- *In the* **Orientation** *area,* Portrait *is the normal way up; use* Landscape *if you want to print with the paper sideways.*
- *The* **Margins** *set the overall limits to the printable area. You can use the indents to reduce the width of text within the margins, but you cannot extend out beyond them.*

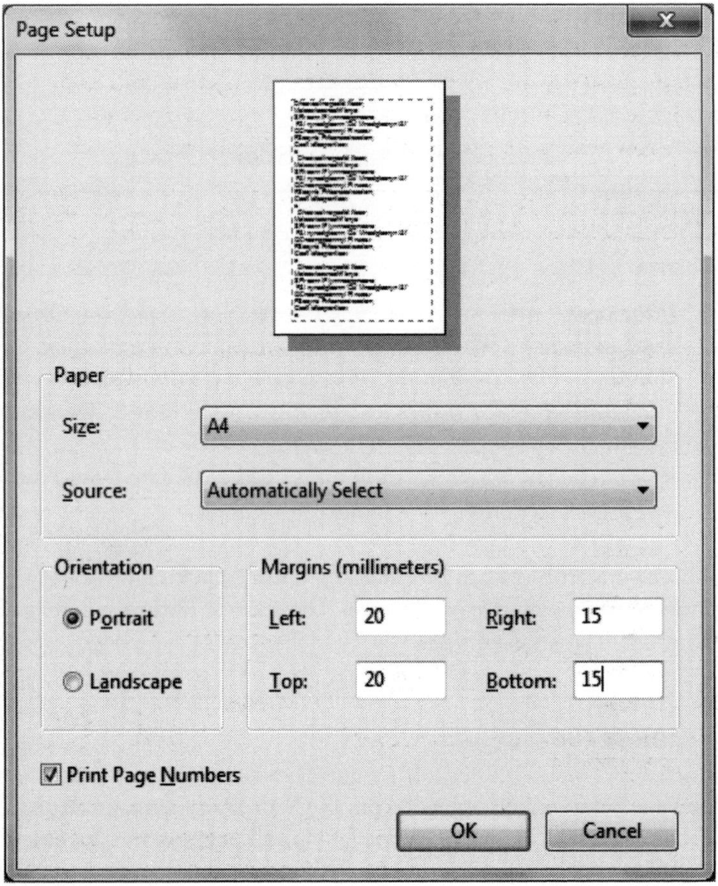

Figure 12.7 The Page Setup panel in WordPad. Measurements here are in millimetres, but can be changed on the View tab.

PRINTING

If you want a single copy of the current document, using the default settings on the default printer, use the Quick Print option in the WordPad menu or the Quick Print icon on the Quick Access Toolbar. For more control over the printing, use the Print command.

Print settings

The Print command opens the Print dialog box where you can specify which printer to use (if there are more than one), which pages to print and how many copies. Click the Preferences button if you want to specify the quality of the print – you might, for example, want to switch to a lower resolution for a draft copy, or a higher resolution for the final output. (At low resolution, the printer will work faster and use less ink or toner.)

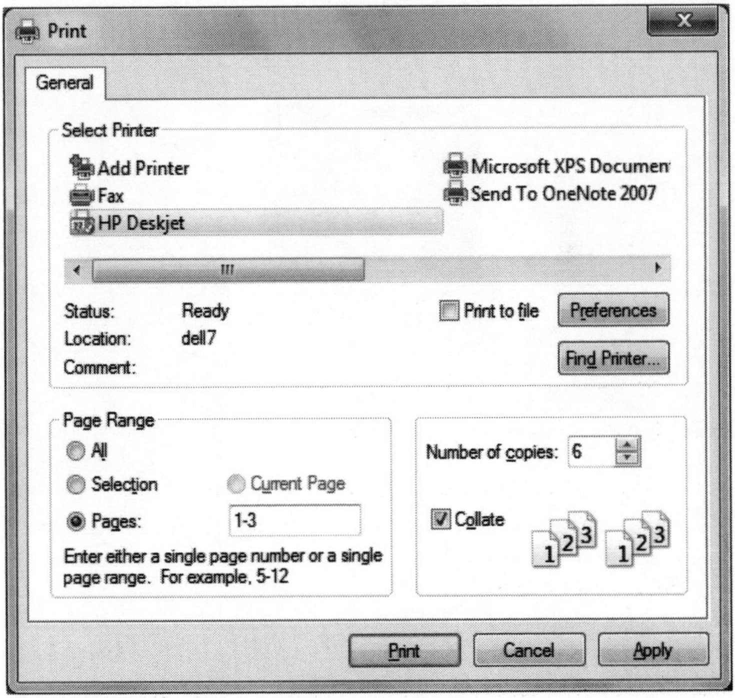

Figure 12.8 The Print dialog box. If you are printing several copies of a multi-page document, make sure that collate is ticked, otherwise you will have to sort each set by hand afterwards!

Print Preview

Like almost all applications, WordPad has a Print Preview facility.
Working on screen, it can be difficult to tell how a document will
look on paper – you may not be able to see the full width of the
page and you certainly won't be able to see the full height. Use
the Preview to get a better idea of the printed output, before you
commit it to paper. Are your images or headings large enough to
make the impact that you want? Do you get awkward breaks in the
text at the ends of pages? If you are happy with the look of your
document, you can print from here by clicking the **Print** button,
otherwise, click **Close** to return to WordPad for further tweaking.

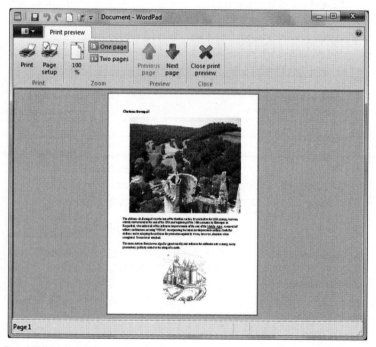

Figure 12.9 Using the Print Preview facility to check the overall layout of a page. You can print from here, or close to return to editing.

SAVING AND OPENING FILES

In WordPad as in all applications you should save early and save often! Don't wait until you have finished writing that eight-page report before you save it. Applications can crash, hardware can fail, plugs get knocked out and we all make mistakes! The first save may take a few moments, but later saves are done at the click of a button.

To save a file for the first time:

1 *Click* the WordPad button to open the *menu and select* Save As...
2 *If the folder shown at the top is not the one you want to use, click* Browse Folders *to open the full dialog box.*

3 *Navigate through your system to select the folder.*
4 *Change the default 'Document' in the filename to something that will remind you what it is about.*
5 *RTF is the standard WordPad format – it can be read by many applications. If you want to save in a different format, pick one from the Save as type drop-down list.*
6 *Click* Save.

7 To resave the current document after you have done more work on it, click the **Save** icon on the Quick Access Toolbar!

When you close the document or exit from WordPad, if you have not saved the document in its final state, you will be prompted to do so.

File formats

WordPad can save documents in several formats:

- RTF (Rich Text Format) is the default, and a good one to use if you are sharing the document with other people. Just about every word processor around can read RTF files.
- Office Open XML document is the format used by Word 2007, and can only be read by WordPad, Word 2007 and some other Microsoft products.
- OpenDocument Text can be read by most modern word processors.
- Plain text saves only the text – not the formatting. Not surprising, this produces the smallest files.

Next time that you want to work on the document, open it from the **WordPad** menu. Either:

- *Select* **Open** *and then browse for the file – the* **Open** *dialog box is used in the same way as the* **Save As** *dialog box.*
- *If it is one of the files that you have used most recently, it will be listed on the WordPad menu. Just select it from here.*

12.2 Character Map

You will find **Character Map** on the **System Tools** menu – don't ask me why! It's a useful tool and one that I like to have close to hand. It allows you to see the characters available in any font, and to copy individual characters from there into a document.

1 *Pick a font from the drop-down list – Symbol, Webdings and Wingdings are the main fonts for decorative characters, and you will find foreign letters and mathematical symbols in most other fonts.*

2 *Click on the character for an enlargement – if you hold down the left mouse button and move across the characters, enlargements will appear as you go.*

3 *To copy characters into a document, click* **Select** *– the current one will be added to the* **Characters to copy** *display – then click* **Copy** *when you have all you want. Return to your document and use* **Paste** *– the character(s) will be copied in, formatted to the chosen font.*

Give yourself an easy link

If you also find that Character Map is a useful tool to have at hand, open the Start menu and drag it from the System Tools folder into the main program list, or create a shortcut to it on your Desktop. Do this with any other Accessories that you find useful.

Click or drag across the display to see an enlargement

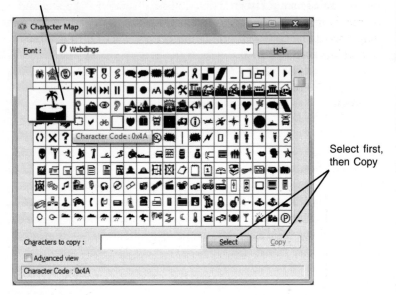

Select first, then Copy

Figure 12.10 Character Map.

12.3 Paint

Graphics software falls into two broad groups. The first type works with objects – lines, circles, text boxes, etc. – that remain separate, and can be moved, deleted, recoloured and otherwise changed at any point. Word's Drawing facility works this way.

In the second type, which includes Paint, the image is produced by applying colour to a background – with each new line overwriting anything that may be beneath. Using these is very like real painting. You may be able to wipe out a mistake while the paint is still wet, but as soon as it has dried it is fixed on the canvas. (though Paint allows you to undo your work.) I use Paint regularly – it's ideal for trimming and tidying screenshots for books, though I don't expect many of you will want it for this purpose. Though it can be used to produce intricate images, these can be created more successfully on a computer art package, with a full set of shading, shaping and manipulating tools. Paint is probably best used to draw simple diagrams, or as a children's toy, or to get an idea of how this type of graphics software works.

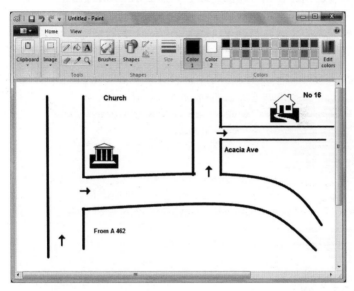

Figure 12.11 Using Paint to create a diagram.

THE TOOLS

The Ribbon holds a simple but adequate set of tools, and shapes, along with options to set the style and thickness of lines, and the colours of the outlines and centres of shapes. A little experimentation will show how they all work.

▶ *The* **Shapes** *button opens a palette of shapes. With most of these you define the shape by clicking to set the position, then dragging to set the size. Immediately after drawing, the shape will still be selected and can be moved to a new place if necessary.*

- ▶ *The outline of a shape will be Colour 1, its centre will be Colour 2. These can be set before or after drawing, while the shape is still selected.*
- ▶ *The* **Brushes** *can be used for freeform drawing, and their styles can be applied to any shape before or after drawing it.*
- ▶ *The* **Size** *options apply to the pencil, the brushes and the outlines of shapes.*
- ▶ *To use the* **Text** *tool – the A button – first drag a rectangle to mark the area, then type your text. A new set of text formatting tools will appear on the Ribbon. As long as the text remains selected – i.e. the dotted outline is in place – the text can be selected, edited and formatted.*
- ▶ *The* **Magnifier** *zooms in 2× each time you left-click. Right-click to zoom back out again.*

Undo it!

If you go wrong any time, use the Undo tool on the Quick Access Toolbar. You can undo any number of things to get back to the last point at which you where happy with your drawing.

WORKING WITH SELECTED AREAS

The rectangular and free-form selectors can be used to select an area of the screen. Once selected, an area can be:

- ▶ **Deleted** *– use this for removing mistakes and excess bits.*
- ▶ **Copied** *– handy for creating repeating patterns.*
- ▶ **Dragged** *elsewhere on screen.*
- ▶ **Rotated** *in 90° increments or* **flipped** *(mirrored) horizontally or vertically – click the Image button and select* **Rotate**.
- ▶ **Resized** *or* **skewed** *– to enlarge, shrink or distort, either horizontally or vertically – click the Image button and select* **Resize**.
- ▶ **Cropped** *– this reduces the canvas to just the selected area. The smaller image can then be saved as a file in the usual way.*

COLOURS

The colour palette is used in almost the same way in all Windows programs. You can select a colour from the basic set – use the left button for the foreground colour and the right button for the background – or you can mix your own colours.

▶ Click the **Edit Colors** *button to open the* **Edit Colors** *panel.*
▶ *To define a new colour, drag the cross-hair cursor in the main square to set the Red/Green/Blue balance and move the arrow up or down the right-hand scale to set the light/dark level. Colours can also be set by typing in values, but note that you are mixing light, not paint. Red and green make yellow; red, green and blue make grey/white; the more you use, the lighter the colour.*
▶ *When you have the colour you want, click* **Add to Custom Colors.** *The new colour will replace the one currently selected in the Color Box on the main screen.*

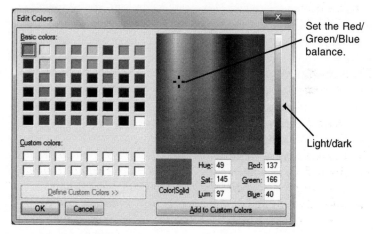

Figure 12.12 Editing colours in Paint.

Saving and opening files is the same here as in WordPad, though here the button which opens the menu is called the Paint button!

Screenshots

If you press the [**Print Screen**] key, the whole screen display will be copied into the Clipboard. If you press [**Alt**] + [**Print Screen**] then only the active window will be copied. The image can then be pasted into Paint, or any other graphics program, and saved from there. That's how most of the screenshots were produced for this book.

12.4 The Snipping Tool

Here is an alternative to Print Screen and Paint. Snip allows you to capture images – the whole screen, a window, any rectangular section, or an irregular shape defined by hand. You can then add highlights or drawn lines on the captured image before saving it or sending off by e-mail. The ability to capture a defined area, and to add highlights, could be useful at times.

To capture a screenshot:
1 *In the* **Start** *menu, open the* **Accessories** *folder and select* **Snipping Tool**.
2 *Click the arrow beside* **New** *and select the* **Snip mode** *from the drop-down list. Then ...*

3 *With a* **Rectangular** *or* **Free-form Snip,** *use the mouse to define the area to be captured.*
4 *With a* **Window Snip,** *click on the window to be captured.*
5 *With a* **Full-screen Snip** *the screen is snipped immediately.*
6 *In the Snipping Tool window, use the* **Highlighter, Pen** *or* **Eraser** *as required to identify or edit points of interest.*
7 *Click the tools or use* **File > Save As,** *to store the image, or* **File > Send To,** *to pass it to someone else.*
8 *Click the* **New** *tool or use* **File > New** *to capture another.*

Snip Options

If you are going to use Snip regularly, check the Options and make sure that it is working the way that suits you best.

Snipping Tool Options   ✕

Application
☐ Hide instruction text
☑ Always copy snips to the Clipboard
☑ Include URL below snips (HTML only)
☑ Prompt to save snips before exiting
☐ Show screen overlay when Snipping Tool is active

Selection
Ink color: ▮ Red   ▾
☐ Show selection ink after snips are captured

                              OK   Cancel

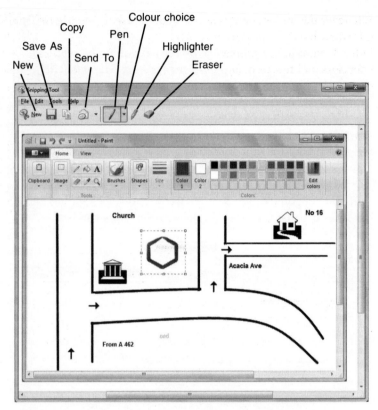

Figure 12.13 The Snip window, here being used to capture a Paint window.

12.5 Calculator

Pack away that pocket calculator. You don't need it on your desk now that you have one on your Desktop!

The Calculator can work in four modes – Standard, Scientific, Programmer or Statistics, and has functions for converting between different units, calculating dates, mortgage repayments, etc. Use the View menu options to switch between them.

Whatever the mode, use this as if it was a hand-held calculator. Enter the numbers, arithmetic operators and functions by clicking on the screen keys, or from your keyboard. (There are a whole bunch of keyboard shortcuts – look them up in the Help file if you prefer keys to the mouse.)

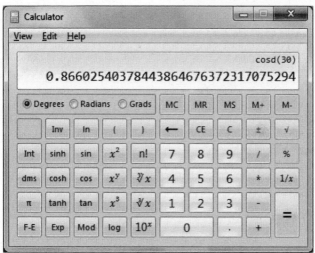

Figure 12.14 The Calculator in scientific mode. In any mode, it works to 32-digit accuracy – is that close enough for you?

It has the same limitations as a pocket calculator – you can only store one value in memory at a time (**MS** to store it, **M+** to add to the value in memory, **MR** to recall it and **MC** to clear it); and you cannot print your results (though you can copy the result into another document). If you want more than this, use a spreadsheet!

12.6 Windows Live Photo Gallery

The Photo Gallery is part of the Live Essentials package, and so not necessarily on your system – though I suspect most people will download the package if only to get Live Mail. It is a viewer for photos and similar image files, but not just a viewer – you can also edit images and add tags or change the star ratings.

It has two modes:

▶ *It can show the contents of a folder in almost exactly the same way as Windows Explorer. The main difference is that tags are also used to allocate images to folders.*
▶ *It can be used to view and edit single images. The editing tools are limited, but effective and all that many of us need to tweak photos before printing. You can adjust the exposure, colour balance and 'red eye', or crop out a section.*

To start Photo Gallery:
  1 *Click on its entry in the Start menu, in the Windows Live group.*
Or
  2 *Open the folder in Explorer, and double-click on an image, to open it in the* **Photo Gallery.**

Fix = go to editing mode   Info = display file information

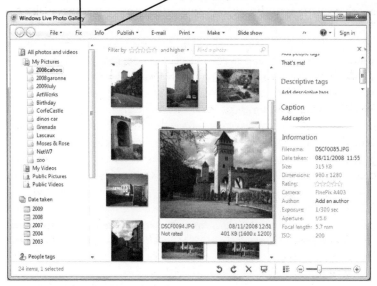

Figure 12.15 The Photo Gallery when exploring a folder.

Revert to folder view

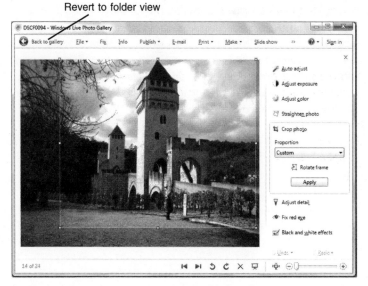

Figure 12.16 ... when working on one image – try Auto adjust before fiddling with the adjustments yourself. It's good.

12.7 Media Player

Media Player is a multi-purpose audio/video player. It can handle
sound files in MIDI and in the native Windows format, WAVE –
as well as audio CDs – or video in the standard Video for
Windows (AVI), Media Audio/Video (WMA and ASF) or the
many ActiveMovie formats.

If you simply want some music while you work, Media Player can
play a CD for you.

▶ *Put the CD into the drive and wait for a moment for Media
Player to start up and to read in the track information. The
CD will play the tracks in their playlist sequence – initially this
will be the standard order.*

RIP AND BURN

But Media Player is more than just a player – it can also rip (copy
music from a CD or video from a DVD) and burn (copy files onto
a CD or DVD). At the simplest you could rip an entire CD onto
your hard drive, then burn the tracks in their original order onto a
blank CD, then wipe the files from your hard drive. But you aren't
restricted to disk-to-disk copying. In between ripping tracks and
burning them, you can edit the information, store the files on your
hard drive and organize them how you like.

Shuffle   Repeat   Play controls   Volume

Figure 12.17 Media Player ripping tracks from a CD.

Respect copyright

As long as you have paid for an audio or video file, or if its authors have waived copyright, then you can make copies for your own use – but not for sale or rental or any other form of earning money.

To rip a CD:
1 *Place the CD in the drive. Windows Media Player should start to play it automatically.*
2 *Clear the checkboxes for any tracks you do not want to rip.*
3 *Click the* **Rip Settings** *button and set the format and bit rate.*
4 **Windows Media Audio** *is the default format. You also have:*
5 **Media Audio Pro** *is designed for use on mobile phones;*
6 **Media Audio variable bit rate** *produces smaller files but takes longer to rip;*
7 **Media Audio Lossless** *gives best quality sound, but at the cost of larger files;*
8 **MP3** *and* **WAV** *formats are available if wanted.*

9 *Set the bit rate, as required – increasing the rate improves the sound quality and produces larger files.*

10 *Start the rip and wait. It'll take a while.*

Rip to a player or a stick

You can rip files directly to an MP3 player. You can also rip to a flash memory stick, which can then be plugged into any audio player with a USB slot.

To edit the album information:

1 *Click the **Library** button and select the album.*

2 *If Media Player cannot read the album and track information from the CD, you will have to supply them yourself. Click into an '**Unknown...**' box and type in the data.*

To burn a CD:

1 *Click the **Burn** button. A Burn List will appear at the bottom right of the window.*

2 *Drag tracks from the Library into the Burn List.*

3 *To change the order of tracks in the list, drag them up or down as required.*

4 *When you have all the tracks in place, click **Start Burn**.*

Figure 12.18 Adding tracks to the list before burning a CD.

Media Center

Windows Media Center is a more sophisticated alternative to the Media Player. As well as playing CDs and DVDs, this can also play recorded TV, if the necessary video decoders and cards are present in the PC.

THINGS TO REMEMBER

▶ *WordPad has enough formatting and layout facilities to cope with many word-processing jobs.*

▶ *Character Map will let you see characters in any font. You can copy them here and paste them into documents.*

▶ *Paint is a simple graphics program that can be used for creating diagrams, fun pictures and for editing and saving screenshots.*

▶ *The Snipping Tool is designed for capturing whole or partial screenshots.*

▶ *Calculator will do the job of a simple (or sophisticated) pocket calculator.*

▶ *Use the Photo Gallery to view and edit your digital photographs.*

▶ *Media Player can play audio CDs, and audio and video files in most formats, and can rip and burn CDs.*

SELF TEST

1 *How do you start WordPad?*

2 *What could you use WordPad for?*

3 *What is the Character Map?*

4 *Can you edit elements of a Paint picture after it is finished?*

5 *What is the Snipping Tool used for?*

6 *Can you operate the Calculator using only the keyboard?*

7 *Why may Photo Gallery not be present on your computer?*

8 *What is meant by 'rip' and 'burn'?*

13

....

Maintenance

13.1 The need for maintenance

Today's hard disks should give you years of trouble-free service.
They will, however, give better service if they are maintained
properly. Windows 7 has tools that do all the donkey work,
once you have started them off – most are designed to be run
automatically. Hard disks are now far more reliable than they were
only a few years ago – it's unusual for them to become corrupted
and lose data, rare for them to crash altogether. But these things
do happen, and files can become corrupted through software errors
or lost through human error. For these reasons, it is important
to protect your valuable data by backing it up – and doing so
regularly.

A disk – hard or floppy – is divided into *clusters*, each of which
can contain all or part of a file. When a file is first written to a
new disk, it will be stored in a continuous sequence of clusters,
and the disk will gradually fill up from the start. If a file is edited
and resaved – bigger than before – it will overwrite the original
clusters then write the remainder in the next available ones, which
may well not be physically next to them on the disk. When a file is
deleted, it will create a space in the middle of a used area, and later
that may be filled by a part of another file. Over time, disks get
messier, with files increasingly stored in scattered clusters.

They are still safely stored, but a file that is held in one continuous chunk can be opened much more quickly, simply because the system does not have to chase around all over the disk to read it.

Disks and drives

These words are often used interchangeably, but strictly speaking, a disk is that flat, round thing on which data is stored, while a drive is a logical area of storage identified by a letter (A:, C:, etc.). The floppy drive or CD/DVD drive can have different disks put into it. A hard disk can be partitioned to create two or more drives.

DISK PROPERTIES AND DISK TOOLS

The key maintenance tools can be run from the Properties panel of any disk. Get to know these, and keep your PC healthy.

Right-click on a drive in Explorer and select **Properties** from the menu, the **Properties** panel will open.

▶ *The* **General** *tab shows how much used and free space you have on the drive – you can run a cleanup from here.*
▶ *The* **Tools** *tab has buttons to start the Error-checker, Disk Defragmenter and Backup.*
▶ *The* **Previous Versions** *tab offers a way to restore files and folders.*

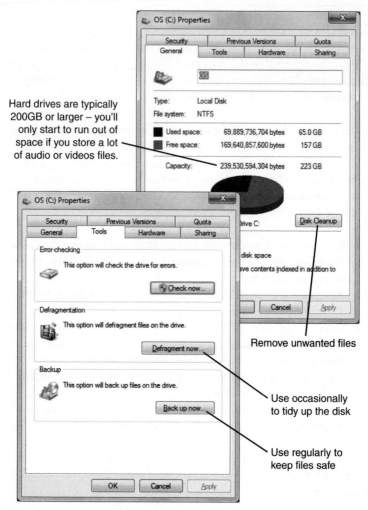

Hard drives are typically 200GB or larger – you'll only start to run out of space if you store a lot of audio or videos files.

OS (C:) Properties

| Security | Previous Versions | Quota |
| General | Tools | Hardware | Sharing |

Type: Local Disk
File system: NTFS

Used space: 69,889,736,704 bytes 65.0 GB
Free space: 169,640,857,600 bytes 157 GB

Capacity: 239,530,594,304 bytes 223 GB

Disk Cleanup

Remove unwanted files

OS (C:) Properties

| Security | Previous Versions | Quota |
| General | Tools | Hardware | Sharing |

Error-checking
This option will check the drive for errors.

Check now...

Defragmentation
This option will defragment files on the drive.

Defragment now...

Use occasionally to tidy up the disk

Backup
This option will back up files on the drive.

Back up now...

Use regularly to keep files safe

OK   Cancel   Apply

Figure 13.1 The General and Tools tabs of the Properties panel of a drive.

13.2 Disk Cleanup

This is the simplest of the system tools, and one that should be run fairly regularly to free up space. It removes temporary and other unwanted files from the hard disk.

To run this tool, click the **Disk Cleanup** button on the General tab of the Properties panel.

When you start Disk Cleanup, if you have an administrator account, you will be asked if you just want to clear your own files, or all potentially unnecessary files. The main types are:

▶ **Downloaded Program Files** *are Java or ActiveX applets (small programs) that you met on Web pages, and which had to be stored on your disk so that they could be run.*
▶ **Temporary Internet Files** – *leave these if you want to be able to revisit pages without having to go online again.*
▶ **Recycle Bin** – *this just saves you having to empty the Bin as a separate operation.*
▶ **Temporary files** *are those created by applications, such as automatic backups and print files. They are normally cleaned up when the application is closed, but may be left behind especially if it ends with a crash. Disk Cleanup will not touch new files, which the application may still be using.*

After you have made your selection and clicked **OK**, you will be prompted to confirm the deletion – this is irreversible – before the cleanup starts.

Figure 13.2 Disk Cleanup.

13.3 Error-checking

In early versions of Windows, the error checking routine was not simple to run, but offered good control of what to do about any errors that it found. The new error checker is far simpler – in fact, it takes total control. All you can do is select the types of checks.

▶ *With* **Automatically fix file system errors** *on, the check will try to solve any problems that it meets – and as it will certainly do this better than you or me, I'd leave it to it!*

▶ *The* **Scan for and attempt recovery of bad sectors** *will fix file system errors and test the surface of the disk, to make sure that files can be stored safely, and rebuild it if necessary.*

The check will be performed the next time the PC is turned on.

1 *Switch to the* **Tools** *tab of the disk's* **Properties** *panel and click* **Check Now...**

2 *Set the options and click* **Start**.

3 *Click* **Schedule disk check** *to run one at the next start up.*

Figure 13.3 Setting up Disk check.

13.4 Disk Defragmenter

We noted earlier that the storage space on a disk is divided into clusters, and that a file may occupy any number of clusters, each linked to the next. On a new, clean disk, each file will normally be written in a set of clusters that are physically continuous on the disk. Over time, as the disk fills up, and as files are written, rewritten (larger or smaller) and deleted, it gradually becomes more difficult to store files in adjacent clusters – the disk is becoming *fragmented*. The files are still safe, but they cannot be read as quickly if the reading heads have to hop all over the disk.

Disk Defragmenter reorganizes the physical storage of files on the disk, pulling together the data from scattered clusters. Though it improves performance, the gains are in the order of a few seconds for starting a program or loading a data file, and it is a very slow job – allow an hour or more on a 200Gb disk. It is only worth doing regularly if your disk is getting full – so that new files are being stored in a limited area – or if you have a high turnover of files from working on large databases or multimedia files, or from installing and removing demos, shareware and other programs.

There is nothing to see when the defragmenter is working, and it works best if the disk is not being used by anything else at the same time. The most efficient solution is to run it on a schedule, at a time when you will not be using the PC.

1 *Open the* **Tools** *tab of the disk's* **Properties** *panel and click* **Defragment Now...**
2 *The first thing to do is find out if it needs defragmenting. Click Analyze disk. If it shows the disk to be more than 10% fragmented (or less if optimum performance is required), then...*
3 *If you are about to end your session anyway, and won't want to use the PC for a while, click Defragment disk.*

Otherwise

4 *Click* **Turn on schedule** *(or* **Configure schedule** *if it is already on).*

5 *Use the drop-down lists to set* **Frequency, Day, Time** *and the* **Disks** *to work on, then click* **OK**.

6 *Click* **Close** *to close the Defragmenter window.*

7 *Make a note of the time and day when you should leave your PC on so that the Defragmenter can run.*

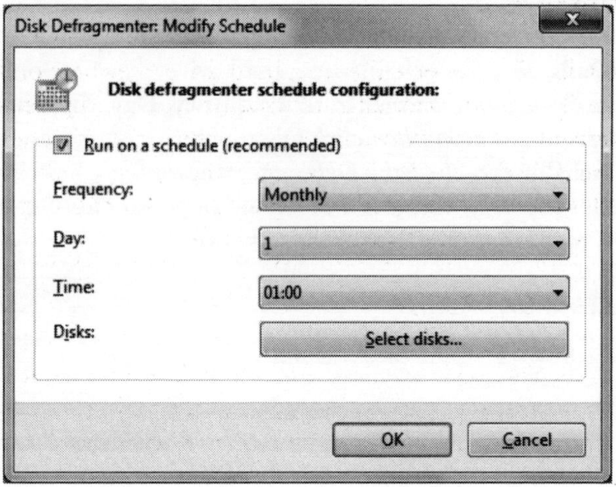

Figure 13.4 Setting the schedule for defragmenting.

13.5 Backup

If an application's program files become corrupted or accidentally deleted, it is a nuisance but not a major problem as you can simply reinstall the application from the original disks. Data files are a different matter. How much is your data worth to you? How long would it take you to rewrite that report, redraw that picture or re-enter the last six months' accounts if they were lost? Individual files can be copied onto floppies for safekeeping, but if you have more than one or two it is simpler to use Backup. A backup job is easily set up, doesn't take long to run and will more than pay for itself in time and trouble the first time that you need it!

Backup media

You cannot run a scheduled backup to a removable CD/
DVD disc. It must be either to a hard drive elsewhere on the
network or to an external hard drive or tape backup device.
External hard drives are convenient, but the cheaper ones are
less reliable that the hard drives on computers – which is not
much good for backing up! Buy good quality, or run your
own backups on DVDs (see the next tip).

SETTING UP BACKUP

The Backup routine is simple to use. To set it up you tell it where
to store the files, the types of files to be stored and the schedule.
The first time it is run, it will backup everything on the computer.
In later backups it will only store those files that have been
changed.

1 *Make sure that your external hard drive is connected, if you
are using one.*
2 *On the Tools tab of the disk's* **Properties** *dialog box, click*
Backup Now...
3 *Click the* **Set up backup** *link.*
4 *Select where the backup is to be stored. Notice that you can
save onto another PC if you are on a network. This may be
convenient but is only really safe if the backup PC is in a
different building.*
5 *You can let Windows choose what to backup or pick the
folders yourself. It really is best to leave it to Windows unless
you are an experienced user and have special requirements.*
6 *At the Review stage, click* **Change schedule**.
7 *Set the schedule, specifying how often, what day and what
time. Backing up doesn't take that long and won't interfere
much with anything you may be doing – but it will run faster
and more efficiently if the computer is not in use at the time.*
8 *Click* **Save settings and exit**.
9 *Click* **Backup Now** *to run the first backup, or close the
window and leave it to the schedule.*

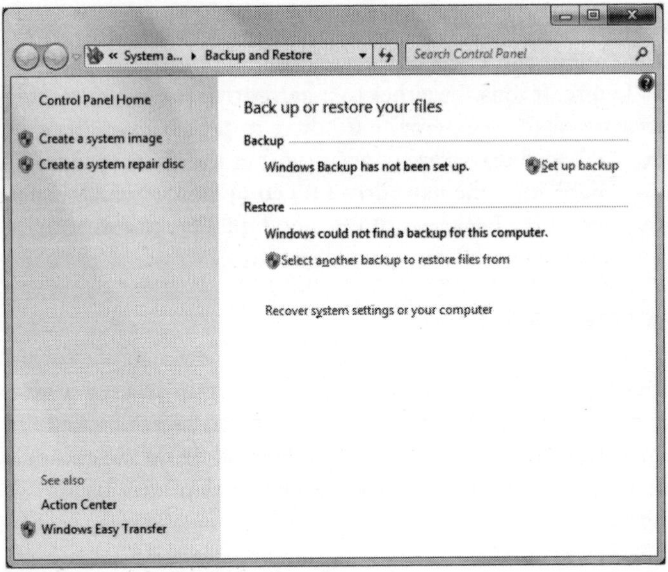

Figure 13.5 Click Set up backup to begin.

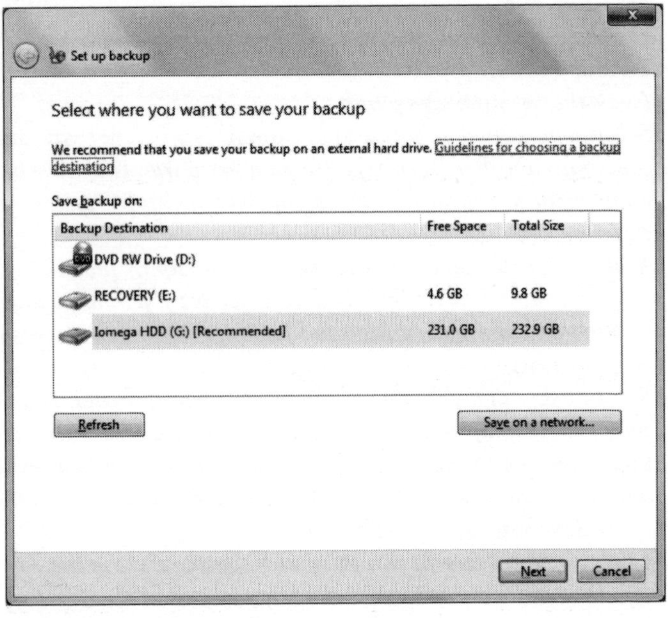

Figure 13.6 Pick where the backup is to go.

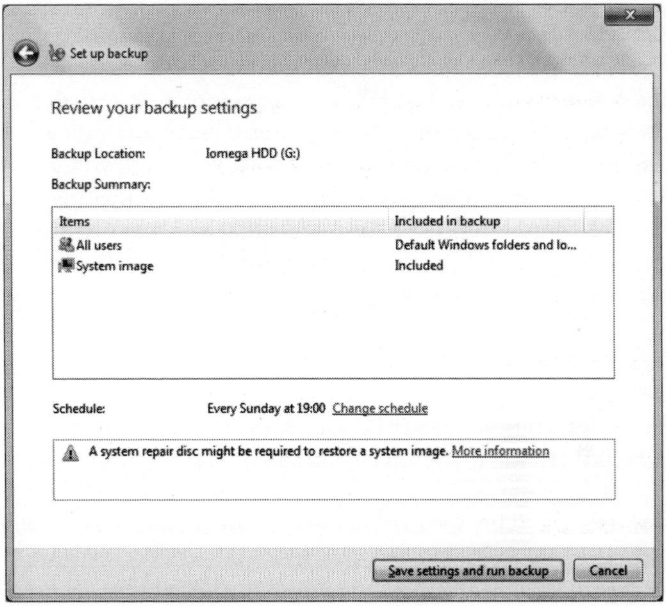

Figure 13.7 Check the settings then turn to the schedule.

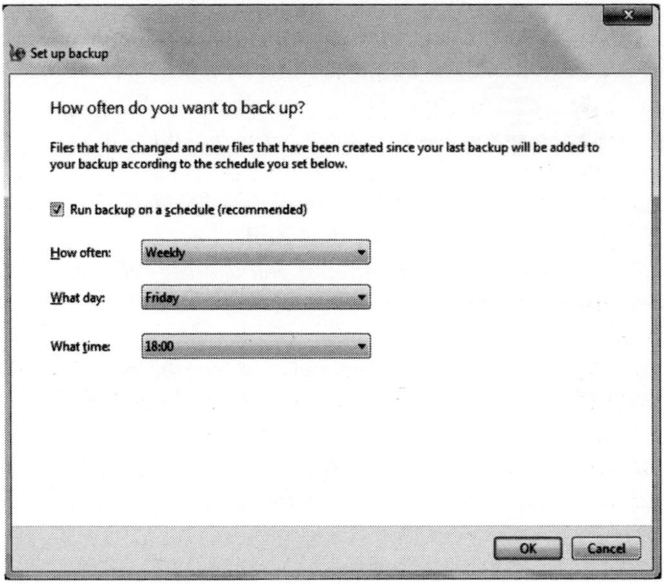

Figure 13.8 Schedule the backup for a quiet time.

Backups on CD/DVD

If you do not have an external hard drive, you can copy files and folders onto a CD or DVD for safekeeping. It is not as efficient as doing a proper backup, nor will it be as simple to restore lost or damaged files, but at least your data will be there. Place a blank or rewritable CD or DVD in the drive and drag onto it those files or folders that you want to keep safe. A CD can hold around 700 Mb of data; a DVD can take around 7Gb.

RESTORING FILES

With any luck this will never be necessary! But it's a straightforward job if you do have to do it.

1 *Make sure that your external hard drive is connected, if you are using one.*
2 *Open the* **Control Panel,** *go to* **System and Security** *and select* **Backup your computer.**
3 *At the Backup window, click* **Restore my files.**
4 *Choose which files to restore – yours or those of all users.*
5 *Click* **Search** *to hunt for files or files by name.*
Or
6 *Click* **Browse for files** *to restore individual files.*
Or
7 *Click* **Browse for folders** *to restore entire folders.*
8 *Locate the files/folders and click* **Add.**
9 *Restore to its original location if you want to replace the existing files with ones from the backup.*
Or
10 *Select a new location if you want to retain the current versions as well – there may be valuable data in the new files.*
11 *Click* **Restore** *to start the process.*
12 *If you are restoring to the original location, and there is already a version of the file, you will be asked if you want to replace it.*

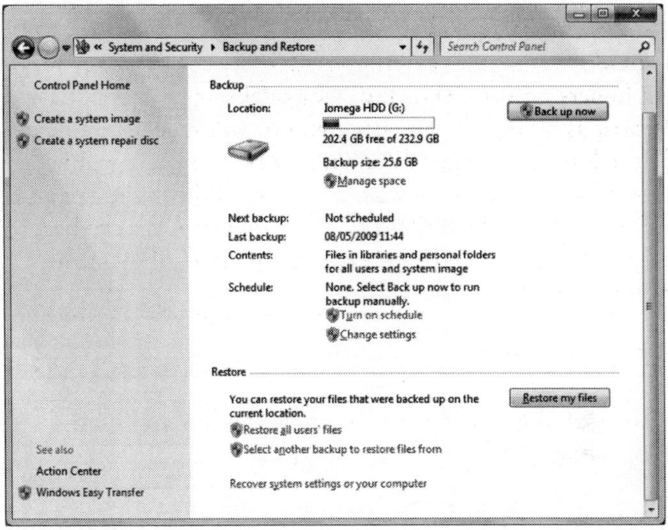

Figure 13.9 Click Restore my files, near the bottom of the window.

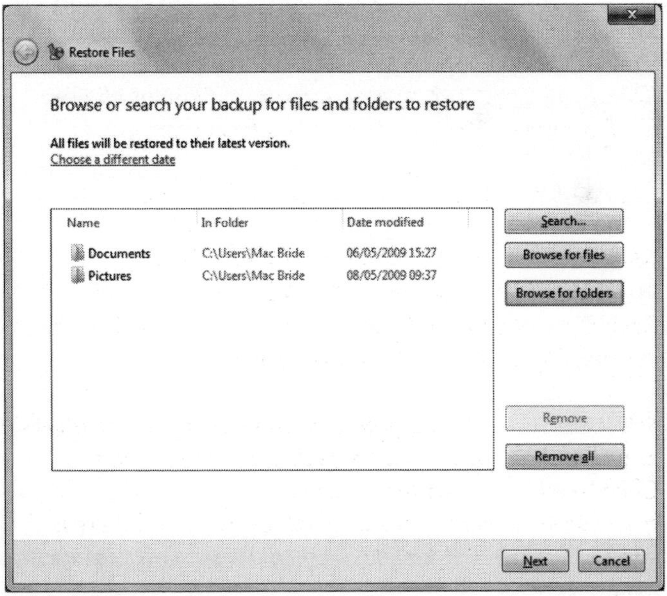

Figure 13.10 Finding the files or folders to restore.

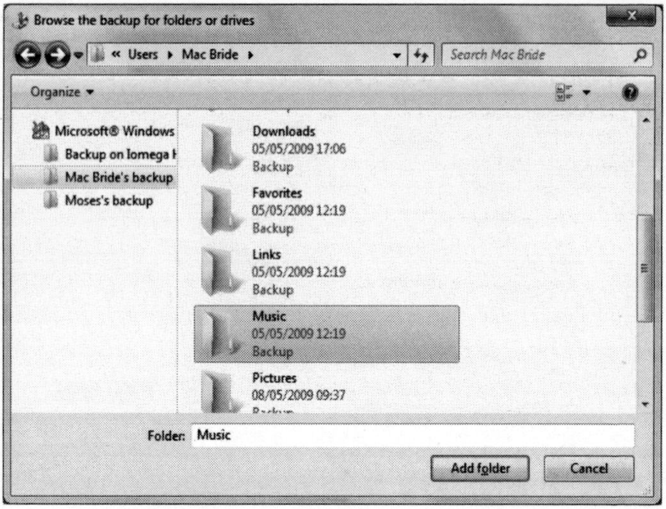

Figure 13.11 Adding a folder to the set.

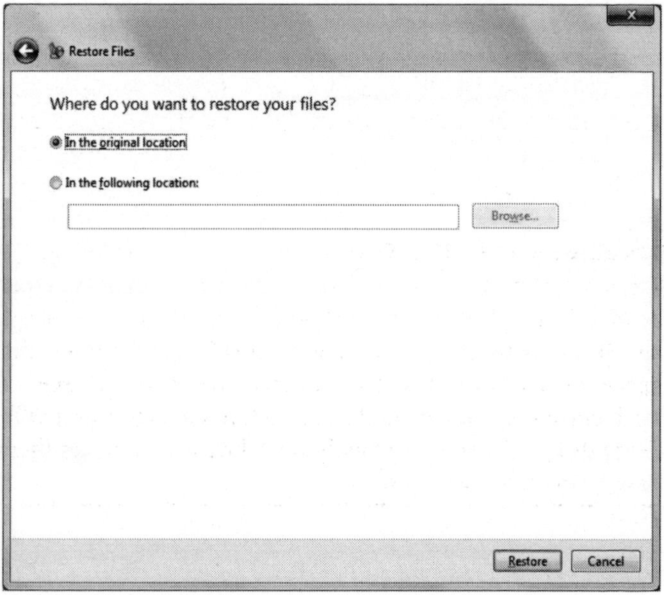

Figure 13.12 Where should it be restored to?

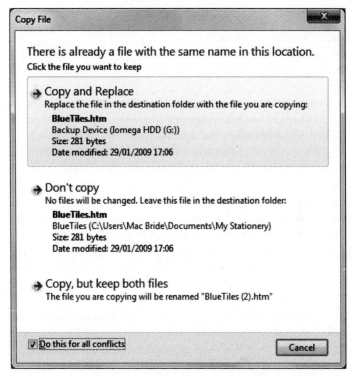

Figure 13.13 When restoring a folder, some files may still be there. You can replace them or keep both copies.

Backup on Flash drive

Flash memory sticks can also be used for keeping safe copies of files. Their advantages are that they are highly portable, reliable, easy to use and you can delete old backups to make space for new ones. The disadvantages are price – an 8Gb stick currently costs around £20, 30 times as much as a 7Gb DVD disk – and they are highly portable, which makes them easy to lose and easy to steal.

13.6 Previous versions

Even if you can't be bothered to backup your files, Windows can. It automatically keeps 'shadow copies' of your files and folders as part of the system protection (see 13.7, *System Restore*), and you can use these to revert to previous versions of files. Use to restore a document or picture after bad editing has made a mess of something good.

1 *Run* **Windows Explorer** *and locate the file or folder that you want to recover. Right-click and select* **Restore previous versions** *from the context menu.*

2 *Find and select the copy from the last time when the file or folder was in the state you want it to be.*

3 *You have three choices. Click:*
   ▷ **Open** *to open a file for reading and resaving, or open a folder so that files can be selected for recovery.*
   ▷ **Copy** *to copy the file or folder to a new location.*
   ▷ **Restore** *to replace the original file or folder with the shadow copy.*

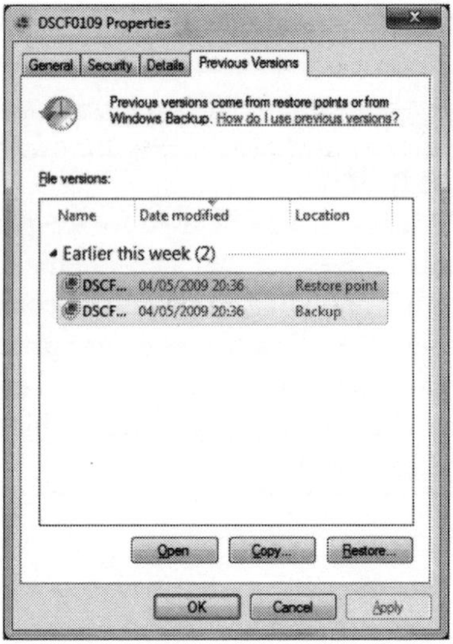

Figure 13.14 Restoring a file from a previous version. Note that you can only do this if System Restore or Backup have been used.

13.7 System Restore

With any luck you'll never need this, but it's good to know that it is there. Windows 7 automatically stores a backup copy of your important system files, known as system restore points, at regular intervals. If these files become corrupted for any reason, e.g. 'user error', new software installation problems or hardware failure, then System Restore will get your system running again.

To restore your system:

1 *Save any files that you are working on and close any open applications – the PC will have to restart to restore.*
2 *Open the* **Control Panel**, *select* **System and Security** *and click* **Restore your computer to an earlier time.**
3 *Click* **Open System Restore.**
4 *You will be reminded that this operation may remove newly installed software, and given a chance to change your mind. Click* **Next** *to carry on.*
5 *Pick as the restore point the most recent time when you know that the system was running properly.*
6 *Click* **Next**, *then* **Finish** *at the last panel to confirm that you want to run the restore. The PC will shut down, then restart using system files as they were at the selected restore point.*

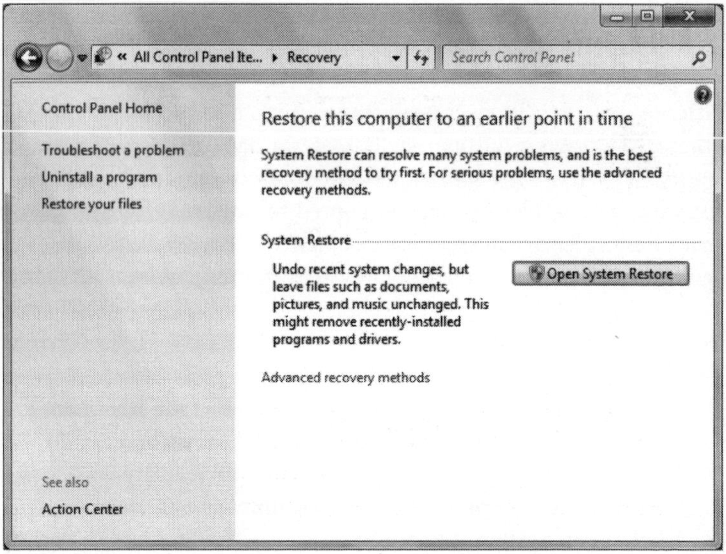

Figure 13.15 Click Open System Restore *to start.*

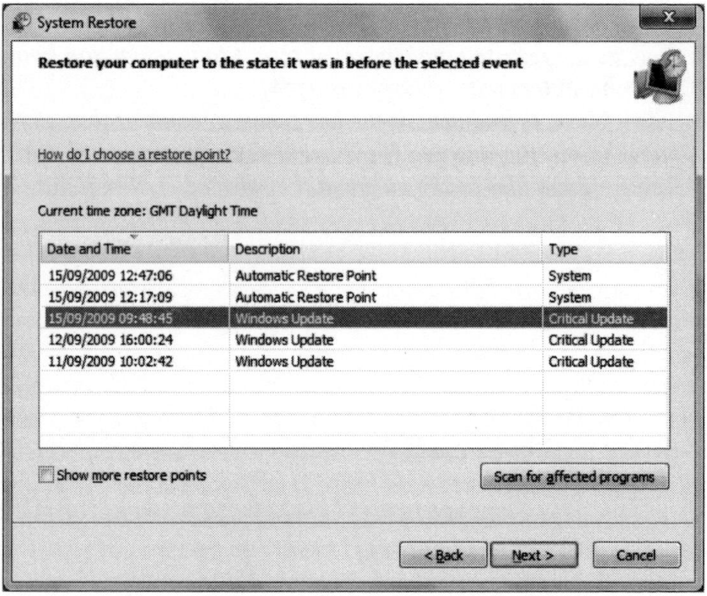

Figure 13.16 Picking a Restore point.

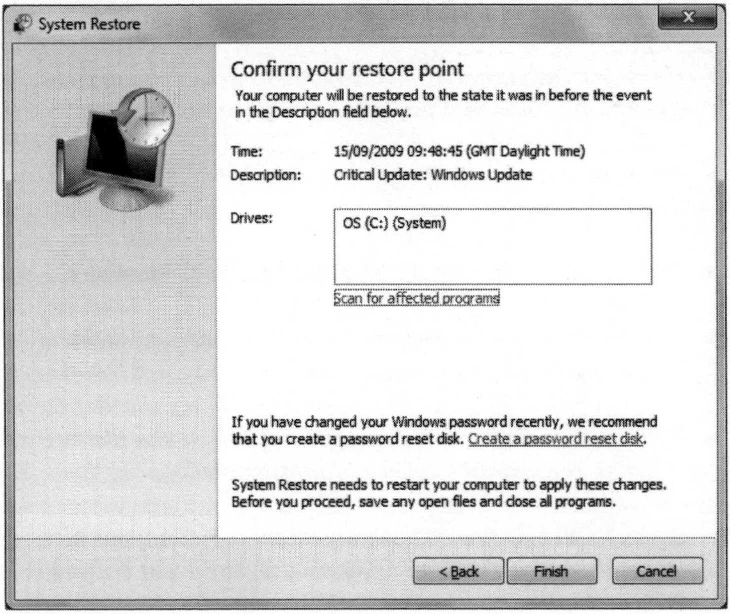

Figure 13.17 Confirming that you want to restore the system.

System Tools

These and other maintenance programs can be found in the System Tools set in the Accessories on the Start menu.

THINGS TO REMEMBER

▶ *Hard disks need regular maintenance to keep them in good condition. Windows 7 provides tools for this.*

▶ *The maintenance utilities can be started from the Tools tab of a disk's Properties panel.*

▶ *Disk Cleanup will remove temporary and unwanted files.*

▶ *Use the error checker regularly to ensure that your files and folders are intact and correctly stored.*

▶ *Disk Defragmenter will reorganize the disk so that files are stored in continuous sequences for faster reading.*

▶ *Backup will help you to keep organized copies of your files. Use it regularly. You may never need it, but if you do, you'll be glad that your backups are there!*

▶ *You can revert to the previous version of a file using a shadow copy stored by the system.*

▶ *System Restore can help to recover the system from calamity.*

SELF TEST

1 *What's the simplest way to access a maintenance program for looking after your disks?*

2 *Why bother with Disk Cleanup?*

3 *What does the error checking routine do?*

4 *How often should you defragment your disks?*

5 *What can I use for backing up files?*

6 *When you try to restore a file to its previous version, you see that there is nothing there. Why might that be?*

7 *When should you use System Restore?*

14

....

Printers

_____

14.1 Adding a new printer

Many printers are 'plug and play' – just connect them, and
Windows will configure the system so that they can be used.
Sometimes you need to install the drivers – the programs that
convert the PC's formatting codes into ones for the printer – and
there is normally software to control and configure the printer.
Here we look at how to manage printers and how to install those
that aren't plug and play.

If your printer dates from before Window 7's release in 2009, the
drivers available in the Windows package will probably be newer
than those supplied with the printer. If it is more recent, dig out its
installation disk.

1 *Click* **Devices and Printers** *in the Start menu. (If it's not there,
open the* **Control Panel,** *and select* **View Devices and Printers**
in the **Hardware and Sound** *area.)*
2 *Click* **Add a printer** *to start the installation.*
3 *At the first screen, select* **Local printer,** *if it is attached to your
PC, or* **Network printer** *if you access it through a network.*
4 *For a local printer, you then choose the port – normally LPT1.*
5 *For a network printer, browse to find the one you want.*

6 To use one of the Windows drivers, select the **Manufacturer** from the list, then the **Printer** model. If an installation disk came with the printer, click **Have Disk.**

7 You may want to edit the full manufacturer/model **name** into something shorter to label the icon in the Printers folder.

8 If you have more than one printer, one is set as the default – the one to use unless you specify otherwise when you start printing.

9 At the final stage, accept the offer of a test print – it's as well to check! Click **Finish** to close the installation window.

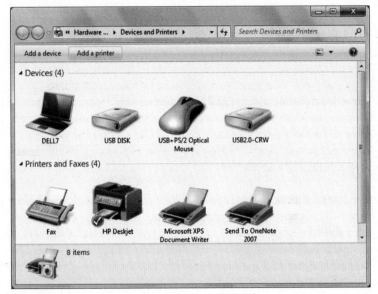

Figure 14.1 Some 'printers' do not actually print. This set also includes a fax and two programs that output the document in formats for use elsewhere.

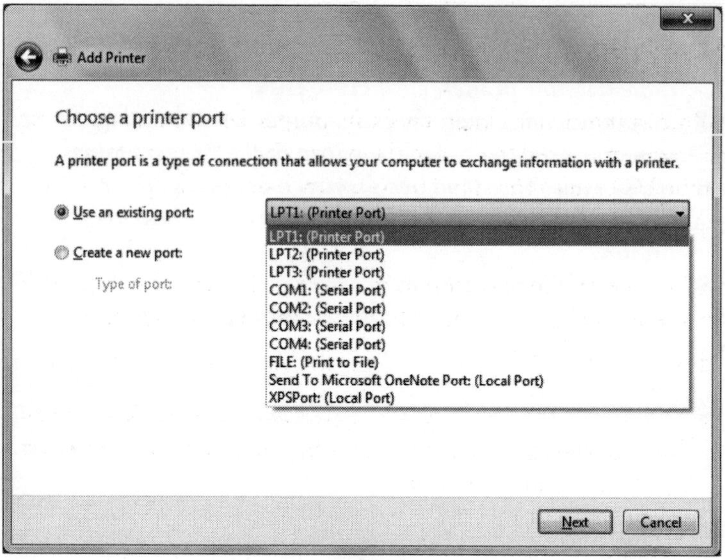

Figure 14.2 Selecting a port. COM ports are used for modems and the like.

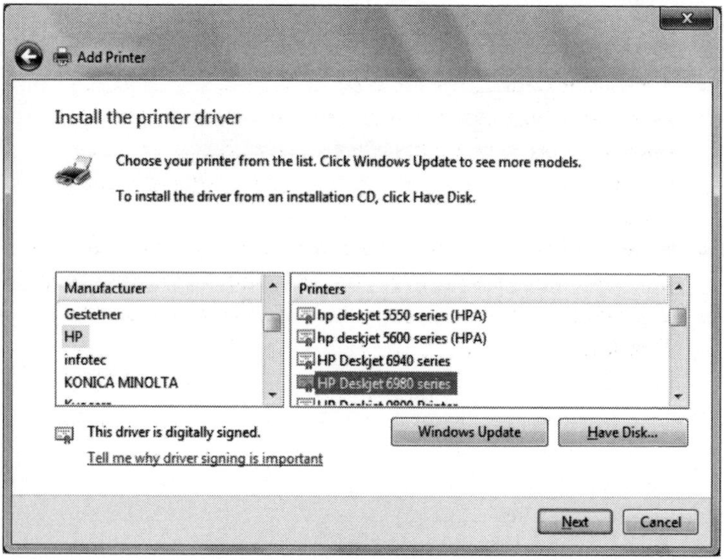

Figure 14.3 Windows has drivers for virtually all printers currently in use.

14.2 Printer Properties

Before you use the printer, check its properties. If nothing else, you may need to change the paper size, as it is often set to the US Letter. The standard UK paper size is A4 (210 × 297 mm).

Right-click on the new icon in the Printers folder and select Properties. Different printers have different Properties panels, but you should find:

▶ A **General** *tab, where you can type a comment. This is mainly useful on a network, to tell others of any special requirements that you or the printer have.*

▶ *An* **Advanced** *tab, where you can select a new driver if needed. The* **Spool** *settings determine whether the file is sent directly from the application to the printer, or through a temporary memory buffer. Spooling frees up applications, as they can generally send data out faster than the printer can handle it.*

▶ *A* **Printing Defaults** *or* **Preferences** *button, which leads to a dialog box where you can set the paper size. The other options here are best left at their defaults, though you may want to change them before printing specific documents.*

▶ *A* **Device Settings** *panel. Check the* **Memory** *(normally only with laser printers). If you have added extra memory – a good idea if you print pages with lots of graphics – tell Windows.*

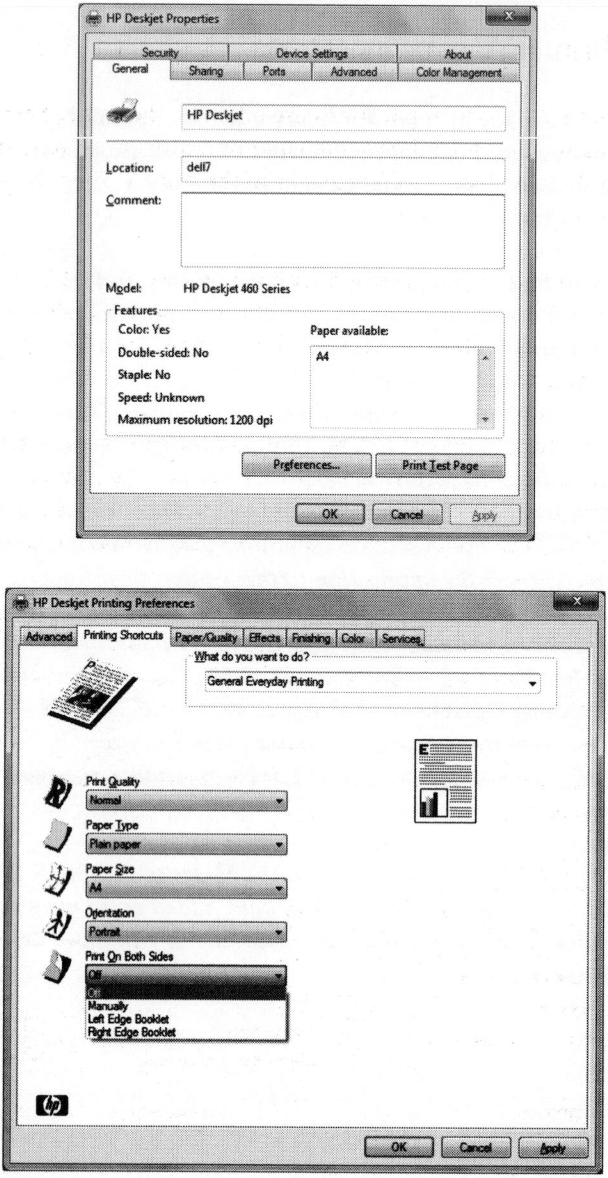

Figure 14.4 The Properties and Preferences panels for a printer. Take time to explore yours to see what options are available, and what defaults have been set – not all may make sense at first! Remember that these are only the default settings, and that they can be changed from within a program before printing a document.

14.3 Printing from applications

The Print routines in applications are all much the same. There will usually be a Quick Print command or a toolbar button, and picking these will send the document to the printer using its current settings – whatever they are.

The first time that you print something, it is best to start by selecting **Print** from the **main** menu. This will open a dialog box where you can define the settings – the key ones are which pages to print and how many copies.

If you need to change the layout, print quality or other printer settings, clicking the **Properties** button will open the printer's properties panel – this may look slightly different from the panel opened from the Printers folder, but gives you access to the same settings.

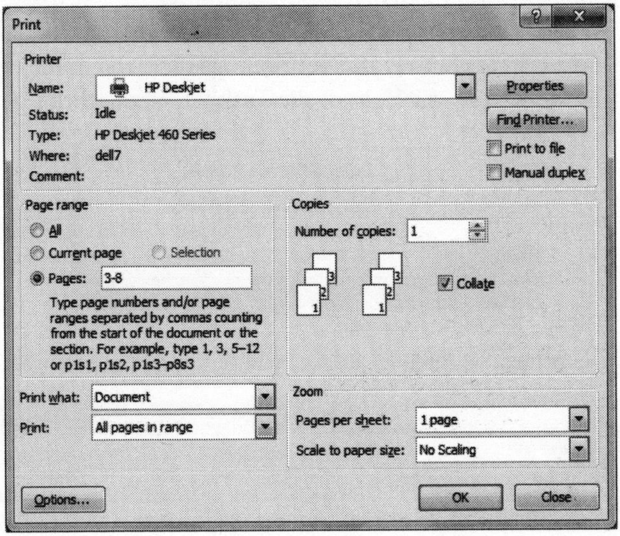

Figure 14.5 The Print dialog box from Word. Other applications have different options, but Page range and Copies are common to all. Note the Collate option. When you print multiple copies, turning this on may make printing take longer, but you won't have to sort a pile of paper afterwards.

14.4 Controlling the print queue

Unless you are very disorganized or have unreliable hardware, most of your printing will run smoothly. But things go wrong even at the most organized and best equipped desk, and problems between printers and PC are not uncommon.

When a document is sent for printing, it goes first to the print queue. If it is the only print job, it is then processed directly. If not, it will sit in the queue and wait its turn. As long as a document is still in the queue, you can do something about it – but if it is just one short, simple document, it will almost certainly be through the queue before you can get to it.

▶ *If you discover a late error, so that printing is just a waste of paper, a job can be cancelled.*
▶ *If you have sent a series of documents in succession, you can change the order in which they are printed.*

When the printer is active, you will see a printer icon in the Notification Area on the right of the Taskbar. Right-click on it.

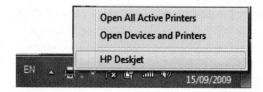

Select the printer to open its folder, where the queue is stored.

Document Name	Status	Owner	Pages	Size	Submitted
Microsoft Word - Dear Gordon		Mac Bride	1	10.2 KB	10:01:02 15/09/2009
Microsoft Word - TYWindows7	Error - Printing	Mac Bride	2	128 KB	09:58:53 15/09/2009

2 document(s) in queue

▶ To cancel a print job, *select the document, then use* **Cancel** *from the* **Document** *menu.*

Document
Pause
Resume
Restart
Cancel
Properties

▶ To cancel all the queued jobs, *use* **Cancel All Documents** *from the* **Printer** *menu.*
▶ *Use* **Pause Printing** *if you need time to restock the paper or replace the ink or toner.*
▶ To change the order of printing, *select a document and drag it up or down the queue as required – this only works with those documents that are not already being spooled or printed.*

Printer
Connect
Set As Default Printer
Printing Preferences...
Update Driver
Pause Printing
Cancel All Documents
Sharing...
Use Printer Offline
Properties
Close

Don't just turn off!

Turning off the printer will stop the printing for the moment, but is not enough to stop a print job. If the document is partially printed or waiting in the queue it will start to print again as soon as the printer is turned back on – and if partially printed, the output when it restarts will be probably be garbled. You must clear the queue to get rid of a print job.

14.5 Printing from file

You can print a document from Windows Explorer, as long as you have an application which can handle it. Windows will open the application, print the document, then close the application for you.

To send the document to the default printer:

▶ *Select the file and click the* **Print** *button on the toolbar.*

Or

▶ *Right-click on the file and select* **Print** *from the short menu.*

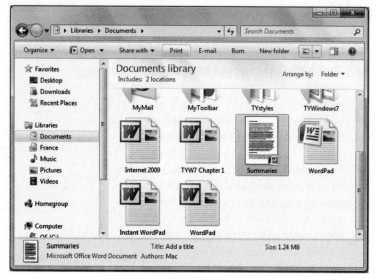

Figure 14.6 You can print a document directly from file.

THINGS TO REMEMBER

▶ To install a new printer, use the Add Printer routine in the Printers folder. Windows 7 has drivers for almost every known printer model.

▶ Check the printer's Properties panel before use, to make sure that the default settings – especially the paper size – are suitable.

▶ When printing from an application, you can usually set the page range and number of copies. If required, the printer Properties can be adjusted before printing.

▶ Documents are taken to the print queue before output. By opening the queue you can cancel a print job or change the order in which they are printed.

▶ A document can be printed directly from Windows Explorer.

SELF TEST

1 *What is a printer driver?*

2 *When might you need to use the Add Printer routine?*

3 *What do you need to check before you use a printer for the first time?*

4 *What is the point of the Collate option?*

5 *If you want to stop a document from printing, or the paper has jammed and you need to stop it, what do you do?*

6 *Do you have to open a document in its application to be able to print it?*

Answers

1 *The left mouse button selects; the right button opens the shortcut menu.*
2 *F1 opens the Help system in most applications.*
3 *The Start menu adapts to each user, displaying the applications that they work on most.*
4 *Press the Alt key to operate the menus from the keyboard.*
5 *With a set of checkboxes, they can all be turned on or off independently of each other. With a set of radio buttons, only one in the set can be on at any time.*
6 *Select the Log Off or Switch User option.*

CHAPTER 2

1 *Windows is an operating system.*
2 *A document is a data file produced by an application, as distinct from executable files which are applications or parts of applications.*
3 *From a Taskbar button or the front page of the Start menu.*
4 *The application will prompt you to save your work.*
5 *The extension identifies the type of file.*
6 *When a program crashes, Task Manager can usually shut it down.*

CHAPTER 3

1 *The screen modes are Minimize, Restore and Maximize. Use the buttons at the top right, or the Control menu to change modes.*
2 *The Cascade Windows command is in the right-click menu that opens from the Taskbar.*

3 *Use [Tab] either with [Alt] or with the [Windows] key to switch between windows.*

4 *Click and drag on the Title bar to move a window.*

5 *Closing a window shuts down the application that was running in it. Use the Close button, the Control menu or [Alt] + [F4] to close.*

CHAPTER 4

1 *You can select a block of text or set of objects by clicking at the start, holding down [Shift] and clicking at the end.*

2 *You can select scattered objects by holding down [Ctrl] while you click on them.*

3 *The Clipboard is a special part of Window's memory in which Cut or Copied data is stored. It can only hold one thing at a time, though that 'thing' might be a group of files or a mixture of graphics and text in a document.*

4 *If you drag a file from Windows Explorer and drop it onto an application that can handle it, the file will open.*

CHAPTER 5

1 *On the Start menu, click Help and Support.*

2 *Start with Windows Basics.*

3   **a** *The heading leads to a set of articles*

    b *Clicking on the text will display an explanation of it.*

    c *Clicking on the heading will open up a detailed list.*

4 *Non-Windows Help systems often have an index.*

5 *A Tooltip tells you what a tool does. It appears if you point at the tool and wait a moment.*

CHAPTER 6

1 *Right-click anywhere on the background of the Desktop and select Personalize from the menu.*

2 *The theme sets the background, colour scheme, sounds and mouse pointers.*

3 *You can set the transparency level in the Window Color routine.*

4 If you select several images for the background, they will
   change automatically, at whatever time interval you choose.
5 In an office, a screen saver can hide your screen while you are
   away from the desk, otherwise it is just decorative.
6 Right-click anywhere on the background and select Gadgets to
   open the Gadgets window, then select and add new ones from
   there.
7 Point to the gadget and click the Close button in its mini toolbar.

CHAPTER 7

1 The Title bar normally shows the name of the application
   running in the window. It does not in Windows Explorer,
   though the Address bar, just beneath, shows the name of the
   displayed folder or library.
2 The View button and View menu options set the way that files
   are displayed.
3 Folders are created within the current folder.
4 To add a tag, use the Add a tag box in the Details pane. Tags can
   be useful for sorting or filtering files, or for finding lost ones.
5 Hold down [Shift] to select a block of adjacent files, or [Ctrl]
   to select a set of scattered files.
6 A file extension consists of three or four letters after the main
   part of the name. It identifies the type of file.
7 To send a file by e-mail, right-click on it, point to Send to in
   the shortcut menu and select Mail recipient. The file will be
   passed to your e-mail software, and attached to a message,
   ready for sending.
8 Restore the deleted file from the Recycle Bin.
9 Click into the Search box and type in something to identify it –
   part or all of its filename, or a tag, or word(s) that you know
   are in its text.

CHAPTER 8

1 The Internet refers to the computers, networks, connections
   and the communications software. The World Wide Web is
   one way in which people share ideas and services over the
   Internet.

2 *Click the Tools button and select Options to start customizing Internet Explorer.*

3 *Parental Controls can be set to limit the times when the PC can be used; Content Advisor can control the sites that children can visit.*

4 *A search engine is a site where you can search for information stored on pages in the World Wide Web. Google is currently the most used search engine.*

5 *A hyperlink is an Internet address attached to some text or an image. Clicking on a hyperlink will make the browser jump to the linked page.*

6 *If you know the address of a site, you can type it into the Address bar and go directly to it.*

7 *A Favorite is a stored link to a page that you may want to revisit.*

8 *To save an image, right-click on it and select Save As. To save text, select it, then right-click on it and select Copy and paste it into a word processor. To save the whole page, open the Page menu and select Save As.*

9 *The Live Essentials package contains some useful programs – you will need Mail, if nothing else.*

10 *Windows Update checks the Microsoft website regularly for bug-fixes (to correct errors in software) and new versions of the Windows programs.*

CHAPTER 9

1 *Live Mail can be downloaded in the Live Essentials package from the Windows Live website.*

2 *A clear Subject line lets people know what to expect in your message and makes it easier for them to find it later in amongst all their other mail.*

3 *People in the Cc and Bcc boxes get a copy of the message, but Bcc addresses are not listed in the headers for other people to see.*

4 *Click the Add Contact link beside their address in the header of the message.*

5 *Click the icon by the To: box to open the Send e-mail window, where your contacts are listed.*

6 When you delete a message it is moved to the Deleted Items box. It can be recovered until it is deleted from there, or until the Deleted Items folder is emptied.

7 Set the option on the Send tab to control whether or not to include messages in a reply.

8 Photos are reduced in size when added to the body of a message, but are sent unchanged as attachments.

CHAPTER 10

1 You can view by category, or icons. Switch between them by selecting from the options on the View by list.

2 In the Control Panel, from the Programs category, click Uninstall a program. Locate the unwanted program and click the Uninstall button.

3 You can change the mouse's response speeds, the icons used for pointers and the way the pointer behaves.

4 Open the Date and Time dialog box, either from the Control Panel or from the clock's shortcut menu.

5 The Magnifier will give an enlarged view of the screen.

6 A Standard user cannot install or uninstall software, or change other people's user account settings.

7 Use the Parental Controls to restrict a child's activities – and make sure that there is a good, safe password on your own account!

CHAPTER 11

1 Right-click on the Taskbar or Start button and select Properties.

2 Setting the Taskbar on Auto-Hide gives you more working space – and it will pop up again when you need it!

3 The Notification Area is the place on the Taskbar which holds icons for programs that control the hardware and low-level parts of the operating system. These will display messages to notify you when there are problems or tasks have been completed.

4 Toolbars can give quick access to programs or other facilities.

5 You can use the Properties dialog box to control which buttons to show on the right pane of the menu; whether these buttons act as a link or lead to a menu; the number of recently-used programs to display on the left pane, and the number of recently-used files to display for each program.

CHAPTER 12

1 If you have not used WordPad before – or not used it much – you will find it in the Accessories group on the Start menu.

2 WordPad could handle most ordinary word processing jobs, as it can handle formatted text, images and other objects.

3 The Character Map shows what each character looks like in every font. Individual characters can be copied from here and pasted into documents.

4 You can delete or paint over areas in a picture, but not edit lines or shapes.

5 The Snipping Tool can capture parts or all of the screen and save the image as a file.

6 There are keystroke equivalents for all the functions and operations on the Calculator.

7 Photo Gallery is part of the Live Essentials set and needs to be downloaded and installed.

8 'Ripping' copies music files from a CD onto your computer. 'Burning' copies music files from your computer onto a CD.

CHAPTER 13

1 Right-click on the disk in Windows Explorer and select Properties from the context menu. Disk Cleanup is on the General tab, the others are on the Tools tab.

2 A disk can get clogged up with unwanted files – especially if you have had, and deleted, large music, photo or video files. The more there is on a disk, the more likely files are to become fragmented.

3 The error checking routine makes sure that data is stored safely on the disk surface.

4 If the analysis shows the disk is more than 10% fragmented, defragmenting would improve performance. Depending upon how much is stored on the disk, and how actively it is used, it may need doing once a month, or never in the life of the PC.

5 For scheduled backups you should use external hard drives or tape drives, or the hard drives of another computer on the network. For making backup copies of selected files and folders, you can use CD, DVDs or Flash drives.

6 If there is no previous version, either it is a new file, or System Restore has been turned off. Check, and turn it back on if necessary.

7 If your computer is not running properly, or crashes unexpectedly – especially if you have recently installed new hardware or software – restoring it to a point before those changes may well solve the problem.

CHAPTER 14

1 A driver is a program that tells the computer how to code a document in a way that the printer will understand.

2 Windows may not have the drivers for a very new – or very unusual – printer, and so you would have to use the Add Printer routine.

3 Check the Preferences to make sure that the right paper size is selected. You should also check your default print settings.

4 When you are printing several copies of a multi-page document, Collate groups the pages into complete sets. If it was turned off, you would get a pile of page 1, followed by a pile of page 2, etc., then have to sort them by hand.

5 Right-click on the printer icon in the Notification Area to open the printer's control window, and cancel the printing from there.

6 No. You can print a document directly from its file in Windows Explorer.

Index

Credits

Credits